The Afghanistan-Pakistan Theater
MILITANT ISLAM, SECURITY & STABILITY

EDITED BY
**Daveed Gartenstein-Ross
& Clifford D. May**

D1444489

FDD PRESS

A division of the
FOUNDATION FOR DEFENSE OF DEMOCRACIES
Washington, D.C.

For information about permission to reproduce selections from this book,
write to: cstr@defenddemocracy.org, or Permissions, FDD Press, P.O. Box 33249,
Washington, D.C. 20033

ISBN: 978-0-981-97123-0

Joshua T. White's chapter "Pakistan's Islamist Frontier: Islamic Politics and U.S. Policy in
Pakistan's North-West Frontier" is adapted from his 2008 monograph of the same title,
with permission of the publisher. © 2008 by the Center on Faith & International Affairs
at the Institute for Global Engagement.

Daveed Gartenstein-Ross's chapter "Religious Militancy in Pakistan's Military and Inter-
Services Intelligence Agency" is adapted from his article "Fixing Our Pakistan Problem"
in the Spring 2009 issue of the *Journal of International Security Affairs*, with permission
of the publisher. © 2009 by JINSA.

Cover art: Michal Baranski / Shutterstock
Cover design: Spark Design / www.sparkdesign.net

ALSO BY THE AUTHORS

Edited by Daveed Gartenstein-Ross & Clifford D. May

From Energy Crisis to Energy Security (FDD Press 2008)

By Daveed Gartenstein-Ross

My Year Inside Radical Islam
(Tarcher/Penguin 2007)

Homegrown Terrorists in the U.S. and U.K.:
An Empirical Examination of the Radicalization Process
(FDD Press 2009, with Laura Grossman)

Terrorism in the West 2008
(FDD Press 2009, with Joshua D. Goodman & Laura Grossman)

TABLE OF CONTENTS

ACKNOWLEDGMENTS

This book is largely a product of the Foundation for Defense of Democracies' (FDD) 2009 Leading Thinkers policy workshop on Afghanistan and Pakistan. This workshop brought together an impressive array of thinkers representing a true diversity of perspectives, including experts with significant regional expertise, leading academics, military strategists, former intelligence operatives, members of the media, and the ambassadors of Afghanistan and Pakistan. At times participants found great areas of agreement, at times their differences led to sharp exchanges; but the conversation was never dull.

All of the contributors to this volume attended the Leading Thinkers conference, and we would like to thank them first. This book would not have been possible without the excellent chapters we received from Hassan Abbas, C. Christine Fair, Vanda Felbab-Brown, Vanessa Gezari, Sebastian Gorka, Shuja Nawaz, and Joshua T. White. We are grateful to Toby Dershowitz and Alan Mairson of The Dershowitz Group and FDD's Sara Westfall for their thoughtful work on this book's layout and design. Melissa Newberg did excellent work fact-checking the chapters, and Tara Vassefi contributed an important final read through the manuscript to uncover remaining grammatical and typographical errors. Gregg Carlstrom of *Al Jazeera English* also helped to ensure the quality of the final manuscript through his excellent work as our outside reviewer.

This book is a product of the passion, dedication, and intelligence that many at FDD have devoted to the organization's significant projects. Though there are many we could name, we would like to single out executive director Mark Dubowitz and senior vice president of communications and operations Bill McCarthy for their tireless efforts.

We thank the Li Ka Shing Foundation for its generous support for our Leading Thinkers conference series, and this book. And we also extend our heartfelt thanks to Bill Nixon, CEO of Policy Impact, and to his talented staff, for all of their support and effort. Bill is truly an enlightened and visionary Washington figure, and we are grateful for his abiding friendship.

—*Daveed Gartenstein-Ross & Clifford D. May*

Introduction

Military operations in Afghanistan are heating up as I write this. Press accounts suggest that NATO operations in Marjah have met with early success[1]—but the key question in this theater has always been what happens after an area is cleared of insurgents. To that extent, the Obama administration has trumpeted a revised strategy for approaching a war in which the U.S. has been embroiled for more than eight years. But observers across the political spectrum agree that military operations alone are not enough to secure Afghanistan against a powerful insurgency; and moreover, any analysis of the war in Afghanistan that ignores the key role played by Pakistan will offer an incomplete picture. A broader perspective is needed, and this book brings together top minds who can help to provide it.

Afghanistan was supposed to be "the good war," in contrast to the U.S.'s war in Iraq. By 2003, the military was telling American officials that the Taliban were a "spent force," and CIA specialists and Special Forces units alike were being reassigned to the Iraq theater.[2] To say that those early proclamations of victory were premature is an understatement. The failures of the U.S.'s Afghanistan policy over the past eight years should be familiar to most readers, including the diversion of resources to Iraq, international forces that were "poorly configured" for counterinsurgency,[3] lackluster attempts at reconstruction, continuing corruption in Hamid Karzai's government, and the absence of a strategy for dealing with the strategic challenges posed by Pakistan. Due to these problems, commentators speculated that Afghanistan could become "Obama's Vietnam" even before Barack Obama won the 2008 election.[4]

Less than three weeks after taking office, Obama selected former CIA officer Bruce Riedel to lead an interagency group designed to review the U.S.'s policy toward Afghanistan and Pakistan. At the end of March 2009, Obama announced what he called a "comprehensive, new strategy for Afghanistan and Pakistan" in a speech and white paper that endorsed a robust counterinsurgency approach. The embrace of counterinsurgency led to questions about whether Gen. David McKiernan, then the U.S. and NATO commander in Afghanistan, was the right man for the job: his meager troop request led chairman of the Joint Chiefs of Staff Adm. Mike Mullen and defense secretary Robert Gates to conclude that he may not be serious about counterinsurgency.[5]

When Gen. Stanley McChrystal was tapped to replace McKiernan, Gates "asked him to assess the mission and report back within 60 days."[6] McChrystal's assessment turned out to be far grimmer than he had expected before he set out to examine conditions on the ground and write his report. The document that McChrystal produced was leaked to *Washington Post* reporter Bob Woodward within weeks of its delivery to Gates, and one oft-quoted line warned that "[f]ailure to gain the initiative and reverse insurgent momentum in the near-term (next 12 months)—while Afghan security capacity matures—risks an outcome where defeating the insurgency is no longer possible." McChrystal presented three different troop options to President Obama. Though the high number of troops within these three options was reportedly 80,000, McChrystal seemed to favor "the middle option, which recommends an increase of some 40,000 more troops."[7]

Despite Obama's earlier expressed commitment to counterinsurgency, his administration balked. One official told the *Washington Post*: "It was easy to say, 'Hey, I support COIN,' because nobody had done the assessment of what it would really take, and nobody had thought through whether we want to do what it takes."[8] But having the full, concrete costs of a counterinsurgency campaign spelled out was not the only thing that had changed. In late August, a presidential election that was heavily tainted by fraud allegations cast further doubt on Karzai's reliability as a partner. There were also domestic political concerns: concurrent with Afghanistan's flawed elections, a *Washington Post*-ABC News poll showed that for first time a majority of Americans felt the Afghanistan war was not worth fighting.[9] In light of these factors, debate reemerged within the administration over whether a counterinsurgency mission was really the best option, or whether a more limited counterterrorism strategy—which Vice President Joe Biden advocated—might be superior.

On December 1, 2009, President Obama announced the results of this new round of deliberations at a speech delivered at the United States Military Academy in West Point, New York. His administration ultimately settled on counterinsurgency over counterterrorism; it provided 30,000 additional troops that would begin to be transferred out of Afghanistan in July 2011.

Obama's address rightly emphasized that the Afghanistan war is "inextricably linked" to the U.S.'s policy toward Pakistan. The way militants use Pakistan poses numerous strategic problems for the United States. Al-Qaeda and other insurgent groups have for years enjoyed a safe haven in Pakistan's tribal regions from which they launch cross-border raids against coalition forces in Afghanistan. That problem is compounded by the fact that NATO supply lines run through Pakistan, and the pace of militant attacks against supply convoys has been increasing. NATO figures show that from June through September 2009 alone, "more than 145 truck drivers and guards were killed in attacks on convoys and 123 vehicles were destroyed."[10]

Moreover, al-Qaeda's safe haven in Pakistan has implications that reach beyond Afghanistan's battlefields. As the group's core leadership has reconstituted in Pakistan, major terror plots in the West have emanated from the country's tribal regions. Significant elements of two of the largest terror plots since 9/11—the disrupted transatlantic airline plot designed to blow up at least seven airliners en route from Britain to the U.S. with liquid explosives, and the 7/7 attacks on London's transit system that claimed 52 lives—could be traced back to Pakistan. Pakistani training camps have also played a prominent role in several European terror plots, as well as Najibullah Zazi's more recently disrupted U.S. plot.

Though there has long been a chorus of voices proclaiming virtually every time period in the Afghan war to be critical, such claims now have far greater credibility. More troops are being sent to the Afghanistan theater, the on-the-ground strategy is changing, and Americans are now more aware that this commitment cannot be sustained forever.

This book is designed to explore vital aspects of the situation the United States confronts in Afghanistan and Pakistan. In the first chapter of the volume,

Hassan Abbas provides lucid analysis of one of the factors that has helped al-Qaeda gain a foothold in Pakistan: peace deals that Pakistan's government entered into with religious militants in Waziristan from 2004 through 2008. Dr. Abbas's chapter is relevant not only for the historical perspective that it provides, but also because it may help shed light on the way forward following the Pakistani government's recent offensives in the country's tribal areas.

The next two chapters hone in on Pakistan's military. Shuja Nawaz describes the fragility of civilian rule in Pakistan and the country's tempestuous experience with military governance, and argues that the balance needs to be shifted in favor of civil supremacy. And the chapter I contribute examines the history of support for religious militancy within Pakistan's military and Inter-Services Intelligence agency. This historical support for the enemies that the U.S. is now fighting in South Asia—including the institutional culture undergirding it, and the relationships between religious militants and uniformed Pakistani officers that have developed over time—now makes U.S. actions in the region far more complicated.

Yet it is important to note that Islamism in Pakistan is expressed not only with the bullet, but sometimes with the ballot. Joshua T. White provides an in-depth study of the Muttahida Majlis-e-Amal's (MMA) success in the 2002 North-West Frontier Province elections, and the political aftermath. After chronicling commentators' concern that the MMA's victory signaled a "Talibanized" Frontier that would threaten U.S. interests, White concludes that this early narrative was too simplistic. "Rather than acting in the mold of the Afghan Taliban," he writes, "the MMA bent to the exigencies of governance and moderated on a host of policies." Further, it suffered defeat in the 2008 elections. White masterfully chronicles the MMA's rise and fall.

Turning from Pakistan to Afghanistan, C. Christine Fair analyzes the implications that the country's flawed 2009 presidential election will have for the insurgency. Though Hamid Karzai's victory has been settled by challenger Dr. Abdullah Abdullah's angry withdrawal from a scheduled run-off, concerns about the election's fundamental defects remain. Dr. Fair demonstrates how the security situation shaped the election's credibility long before Afghan voters took to the polls, and argues that concerns about Kabul's corruption and ineffective governance could thwart international efforts at reversing the insurgency's gains.

Vanda Felbab-Brown examines another major challenge to counterinsurgency efforts in Afghanistan, the country's large-scale drug economy. Though this illicit economy strengthens the insurgency, Dr. Felbab-Brown warns that aggressive suppression-based counternarcotics policies will not enhance American objectives: in fact, for years eradication and interdiction-based counternarcotics policies paradoxically strengthened the Taliban by creating an opening for it with drug traffickers and giving it access to the population. She outlines a more comprehensive approach for dealing with Afghanistan's narcotics problem.

Vanessa Gezari examines the Human Terrain System in Afghanistan. This effort to embed civilian social scientists with American military units in order to advise soldiers about a variety of factors that might influence the civilian population has been the subject of great controversy, particularly within the academy: the American Anthropological Association came out against the program in 2007, explaining that anthropologists' participation raised serious ethical concerns. Gezari argues that regardless of the fate of the Human Terrain project, the approach it represents will survive. "A growing number of anthropologists and social scientists are working in various capacities to make the military smarter about the people it is fighting among," she writes, "and the military is finally listening."

Finally, Sebastian Gorka concludes the book by arguing that a fundamental principle of any conflict is that strategists must understand the nature of the enemy they confront, and the U.S. has failed in this regard. He compares the current fight against Islamist terrorism unfavorably to the Cold War, where "doctrinal and strategic issues were settled early on by the likes of George Kennan, Harry Truman, and George Marshall," whose prescriptions "remained fundamentally unchanged for forty years and eventually brought victory." Dr. Gorka argues that the United States needs to go on "the ideological offensive."

This collection represents a diversity of political perspectives and policy prescriptions. Nobody believes that the way forward in Afghanistan will be easy, and all official pronouncements portray an arduous road ahead. The need for clear thinking and informed decisions is clear; and in that regard I believe the volume you are holding makes a significant contribution to the public debate.

— *Daveed Gartenstein-Ross*

ENDNOTES

1   See, e.g., "U.S. Says Marjah Operations Going Well," *Associated Press*, Feb. 25, 2010.

2   See David Rohde & David E. Sanger, "How a 'Good War' in Afghanistan Went Bad," *New York Times*, Aug. 12, 2007.

3   Stanley A. McChrystal, "COMISAF's Initial Assessment," Aug. 30, 2009.

4   The earliest such reference that I could find in a major newspaper comes from Arnaud de Borchgrave, "Afghanistan Quandary," *Washington Times*, July 17, 2008. De Borchgrave writes that Obama "says he is prepared to shift a large number of U.S. soldiers and assets to the guerrilla war against Taliban in Afghanistan. That leads some intelligence experts to ask, somewhat anxiously, whether Afghanistan could become Mr. Obama's Vietnam."

5   My discussion of the Obama administration's process of formulating a new strategy for Afghanistan is indebted to Rajiv Chandrasekaran's excellent article on the subject. See Rajiv Chandrasekaran, "Civilian, Military Officials at Odds Over Resources Needed for Afghan Counterinsurgency," *Washington Post*, Oct. 8, 2009.

6   Ibid.

7   Martha Raddatz, "80,000 is the High Number of Troops Options in McChrystal's Request," *The Note (ABC News)*, Oct. 13, 2009.

8   Chandrasekaran, "Civilian, Military Officials at Odds Over Resources Needed for Afghan Counterinsurgency."

9   Jennifer Agiesta & Jon Cohen, "Public Opinion in U.S. Turns Against Afghan War," *Washington Post*, Aug. 20, 2009.

10   Tim McGirk, "Taliban Stepping Up Attacks on NATO Supply Convoys," *Time*, Oct. 7, 2009.

1 | An Assessment of Pakistan's Peace Agreements with Militants in Waziristan (2004-2008)

by Hassan Abbas

In the aftermath of U.S. and allied forces' military campaign in Afghanistan beginning in late 2001, many Afghan, Central Asian, and Arab militants fled from Afghanistan to Pakistan's Federally Administered Tribal Areas (FATA). Local Pashtun tribesmen readily offered them sanctuary, based upon their relationships dating back to the anti-Soviet Afghan "jihad" years, and as per the norms of *Pashtunwali.*[1] Small numbers of Pakistani soldiers on the border could neither halt the inflow of these militants nor curb the outflow of Pashtuns who felt duty-bound to go toward Kabul to rescue their brethren during the U.S.-led campaign. This cross-border movement pattern was predictable in light of historical precedents (e.g., Pashtun movement during Durrani rule and the Nadir Shah era) and given that many Pashtun tribes straddle the Durand line that divides Pakistan and Afghanistan.[2] Such a scenario should have been taken into consideration while the military operation was planned.

Under U.S. pressure, Pakistan's then-president Pervez Musharraf moved a larger segment of troops to FATA in 2003-2004 to counter the influx of foreign fighters, particularly in North and South Waziristan, FATA's two most volatile agencies. These military units were supported by the Frontier Corps (FC), a paramilitary force raised from among FATA tribes which has existed since the era of British rule. The military operations in Waziristan clearly failed to subdue tribes. Having given a very tough time to the Pakistani army, which suffered heavy casualties in the process, the newly empowered groups (mostly Pakistani tribesmen and militants, in collaboration with small contingents of Arab and Central Asian warriors) started altering the traditional power balance in the area: They shifted authority and control from tribal elders (the hereditary *malik* system) to young religious radicals. Behind religious slogans, class battles were also at play. For the past several years, there have been local demands for drastic reforms in the tribal structure against the corrupt and autocratic *malik* system, as maliks were seen as elitist. Historically, maliks have been responsible for distributing financial support to those who remain loyal to the status quo and keep supporting the government of Pakistan. Consequently, when local Taliban, influenced by Afghan Taliban and Arab fighters, rose against the *malik* system and the monopoly of tribal chiefs, they were supported by many in the tribal region.[3]

Inside Afghanistan, the Western nation-building project's inadequacies and limitations led to a resurgence of Taliban in various parts of the Pashtun-dominated south. On the Pakistani side, meanwhile, the Tehrik-i-Taliban Pakistan (TTP) emerged on the scene in late 2007, and since then has wreaked havoc through a series of suicide attacks and bombings in major urban centers. The spillover effect of Talibanization in the North-West Frontier Province (NWFP) was evident from extremism and militancy in the Swat Valley and other parts of the NWFP. Beginning in May 2009, Pakistan's army, with support from the newly-formed democratic governments in NWFP and Islamabad, first moved against militants in NWFP's Swat district with significant firepower and in November 2009 expanded the operation to FATA's South Waziristan agency. Militants in Swat as well as South Waziristan received serious setbacks during these operations, though in both cases many escaped to mountains in the Pakistan-Afghanistan border areas.

The 2009 military operation against the Taliban in Swat and FATA is believed to be the first sustained and effective action on Pakistan's part, after it felt that its own stability was endangered by the terrorist designs of native Taliban elements. In this context, it is useful to study the various "peace deals" that Pakistan negotiated with militants in FATA under President Musharraf during the 2004-2008 timeframe. The apparent purpose of these deals was to prevent the conflict zone from expanding, and to avoid a head-on collision with militants, many of whom had good working relations with the security forces in the past. These objectives were not achieved; in fact, the deals proved counterproductive. Pakistani security analysts, however, maintain that a negotiated resolution of conflict is better than military confrontation. It is worth analyzing these agreements to draw lessons about the future course of action in FATA—both for Pakistan, and for U.S. counterinsurgency efforts.

MILITARY CAMPAIGNS AND "PEACE DEALS"

Pakistan's military launched Operation *Meezan* (Balance) in 2002, thus entering FATA for the first time since the country's independence in 1947.[4] Roughly 25,000 military and paramilitary troops were deployed to FATA at the time. The second phase of deployment and military action began in March 2004, reportedly under intense U.S. pressure, when Pakistan's army launched the Kalusha operation near the Wana area in South Waziristan.[5] It was meant to be a surgical operation targeting militant hideouts, but turned out to be an utter failure when militants responded swiftly and strongly. This was an unexpected blow to security forces, which were not expecting tough resistance.

Pakistan's army responded with indiscriminate bombing, unintentionally helping the militants through the resulting high civilian casualties. Contrary to standard principles of warfare, a peace deal with militants was pursued at this juncture, and was implemented by the military leadership. Pakistan's army was in a weak situation on the ground, and it was an inappropriate time to opt for a negotiated deal. Such deals are better worked out from a position of strength. The details of the agreement make this point clear:

SHAKAI Agreement (South Waziristan Agency). The signing of peace agreements with militants started with the SHAKAI Agreement in early 2004. It was signed with notorious but charismatic militant leader Nek Muhammad and his militant commanders at Shakai, South Waziristan, on April 24, 2004. Nek Mohammad, a Wazir tribesman, was known in the region for his bravery. He was believed to have provided sanctuary to Uzbek militant leader Tahir Yuldashev during the confrontation with Pakistan's army.[6] The agreement's ten signatories from the militants' side were Muhammad Mirajuddin, Maulana Abdul Malik, Maulana Akhtar Gul, Muhammad Abbas, Nek Mohammad, Haji Sharif, Baitullah Mehsud, Noor Islam, Muhammad Javed, and Muhammad Alam (alias Abdullah). Two names are especially noteworthy—Noor Islam and Baitullah Mehsud—as both later emerged as leading militant leaders of the Pakistani Taliban movement. Two representatives of the area in the National Assembly of Pakistan, known for their pro-Taliban leanings, acted as mediators: Maulana Merajuddin Qureshi and Maulana Abdul Malik Wazir. The crucial clauses of the "confidential" agreement are quite instructive (though some claim that the agreement was verbal and not written):

1. The government will release prisoners taken before and during the recent operations in the area. About 163 local and Afghan militants were released under this clause.
2. The government will pay compensation for the "shuhada" (martyred/injured persons) during the operation, and for collateral damage caused during the military operation.
3. The government will not take action against Nek Muhammad and other wanted individuals.
4. The government will allow foreign "mujahidin" (foreign fighters) to live peacefully in Waziristan.
5. "Mujahidin" will not resort to any action against the land and government of Pakistan.
6. "Mujahidin e Waziristan" (fighters from Waziristan) will not resort to any action against Afghanistan.[7]

According to Rahimullah Yusufzai, a leading Pakistani journalist, the agreement was described by both sides "as a reconciliation between estranged brothers."[8] Yusufzai also maintained that General David Barno (commander of the Combined Forces Command in Afghanistan 2003-05) called Peshawar Corps Commander Safdar Hussain to congratulate and thank him for formulating a policy that would isolate al-Qaeda by draining it of its local support in South Waziristan. The arrangement did work for roughly seven weeks, in the sense that there was no flare-up of violence, but soon differences arose as to the interpretation of a clause dealing with the registration of foreign militants.

The government believed that foreign militants were to be handed over to state authorities, whereas the militants argued that there was no specific agreement on this point. When pushed, the militants asked for more time to deliver on this aspect, but clearly they were just trying to gain time. After they missed a couple of deadlines, military operations were re-launched on June 11, 2004.[9] Nek Mohammad was killed by a Hellfire missile launched from a U.S. Predator drone eight days later, indicating that U.S.-Pakistan cooperation was working reasonably well.

The negative consequences of the deal outweighed its utility. Nek Mohammad became a hero in the eyes of local population, and though he was killed after he backed out of the agreement, he created a new model of defiance for young radicals of the area. The recent history of FATA had witnessed many fighters, but hardly anyone had challenged Pakistan's military. In this sense, Nek Mohammad had created a new pattern. Moreover, Pakistan's army faced immense obstacles to re-arresting the militants who were released as part of the arrangement; they went back to their business. At the end of the day, in the eyes of the local population, the militants assumed more importance than the traditional tribal leaders since Pakistan's government had accorded them an elevated status by engaging them in negotiations directly.

Sararogha Peace Deal. The militancy was fast assuming the status of an insurgency during the 2004-05 period, and it expanded from the Wazir tribe of South Waziristan to the Mehsud tribes in the agency. Abdullah Mehsud and Baitullah Mehsud emerged as major militant leaders during these years. Pakistan's government felt it had no option but to try to implement another deal to bring calm in the Mehsud territories. A deal was inked between Baitullah Mehsud and the government of Pakistan on February 7, 2005, at Sararogha, South Waziristan.[10] Learning lessons from the previous deal, a written agreement was signed but not publicly disseminated:

1. Militants (under Baitullah Mehsud) will neither harbor nor support any foreign fighter in the area.
2. Militants will neither attack any government functionary nor damage government property. They will not create any hindrance to development activities.
3. The government will not take action against Baitullah Mehsud and his supporters for their previous activities. Future involvement in any kind of terrorist or criminal activities will be dealt with under the prevailing laws in FATA. Violators of this arrangement will be handed over to the government.
4. Baitullah Mehsud pledged that if any "culprit" (not from his group) was found in his area, the Mehsud tribe would hand him over to government authorities in FATA.
5. All issues not covered under this agreement will be resolved with mutual consultation between the political administration and Mehsud tribe.[11]

The agreement was signed by Baitullah Mehsud and several members of his group: Malik Inayatullah Khan, Malik Qayyum Sher, and Malik Sher Bahadar Shamankhel.

There were major lacunae in this "deal." Interestingly, no clause was inserted regarding cross-border infiltration or attacks in Afghanistan, and no demand was made about the surrender of "foreign militants." Serious controversies also arose during peace negotiations regarding the issue of financial payments to the militants. For instance, Amir Mir, a bold Pakistani journalist, claimed in an *Asia Times* article that "tribal militants demanded Rs 170 million (US$2.8 million) during the course of peace negotiations, and eventually settled for Rs 50 million to repay debts they owed to al-Qaeda-linked foreign militants."[12] The BBC also confirmed such reports, but some sources claimed the money was meant as compensation for property damaged in South Waziristan during the military campaign.[13] In any case, the arrangement clearly strengthened militants' influence and status in the area as they practically won the freedom to expand their activities. It seemed that one could get away with anything in the name of a peace deal.

Two issues are worth mentioning here. First, the Wazir-Mehsud tribal rivalry in the area is entrenched, and Pakistan's army was possibly attempting to widen that gulf by being soft on one tribe. If so, it was a dangerous gamble that failed: the government of Pakistan failed to realize that for both Wazirs and Mehsuds, Pakistan's army was an "outside force" against whom they were expected to join hands. Second, Baitullah Mehsud and Haji Omar, who were the main signatories of the deal, publicly said that they were committed to continuing to wage their "jihad" against the U.S.-led coalition in Afghanistan, and these statements were reported in the mainstream Pakistani media.[14]

The deal was unilaterally scrapped by Baitullah Mehsud on August 18, 2007, in reaction to increased patrols by Pakistan's army. As is evident now, the deal allowed him to become an unrivalled king of the area, and he trashed the deal a few months before he launched TTP. Mehsud was finally killed in August 2009 by a U.S. drone strike.

Mirahshah Peace Acccord. Uthmanzai Wazirs of North Waziristan were the next to revolt, as they started attacking security forces and their convoys regularly.[15] Pakistan's army conducted various limited operations in response, but an insurgency-like situation quickly developed. The two previous "peace deals" had set a precedent: whoever challenges the government writ has more leverage during negotiations. Predictably, Pakistan cut another deal, this time with the militants of North Waziristan on September 5, 2006. There were certainly some improvements in the way the arrangement was negotiated and finalized. For instance, government functionaries who held civilian administrative positions in the area were involved in the process, and a detailed agreement was drafted before the "signing ceremony." Important points of the 16-clause agreement are as follows. First, the Uthmani Wazirs (including local Taliban, religious leaders, and tribal elders) committed that:

1. There will be no attacks on law enforcement agencies and government property.
2. No parallel administrative set-up will be introduced, and the writ of government will be respected. In case of any dispute about the implementation of the agreement, local administration will be consulted to resolve the issue.
3. There will be no cross-border movement to support militancy in Afghanistan. There will be no restriction on border crossing, however, for the purposes of trade/business and meeting relatives according to local norms.
4. Similarly, there will be no support for militant activity in the surrounding agencies of FATA.
5. All foreigners residing in North Waziristan will be asked either to leave Pakistan or to remain peaceful and abide by this agreement.
6. All captured government vehicles, equipment, and weapons will be returned.

In return, the government's promises included:

1. All militants and civilians of the area arrested during the recent military operation will be released, and will not be arrested again on the previous charges.
2. The government will resume providing financial resources to local maliks.
3. The government will remove all newly-established checkpoints on roads, and will also post Levies and Khasadars on the old checkpoints as in the past.
4. The government will return all vehicles and other items, like weapons etc., captured during the operation.

5. The government will pay compensation for all collateral damage to the affected families.

6. According to tribal traditions, there will be no restrictions on carrying weapons, except heavy weapons.

7. Implementation of the agreement will start after all military action is stopped, and after the withdrawal of Pakistan's army from checkpoints to its barracks. However, the government has the right to take action if any group violates the agreement.[16]

On the militant side, the agreement was signed by Hafiz Gul Bahadar, Maulana Sadiq Noor, and Maulana Abdul Khaliq. Some analysts believe that Mullah Omar, the Taliban leader, endorsed the accord and persuaded local militants to sign.[17]

Similar to the Sararogha arrangement, some financial compensation was included in the deal, thus strengthening the militants' influence. Though the agreement was more intrusive about the issue of "foreigners" (meaning al-Qaeda and Central Asian militants), around 100 mid-level Taliban and Arab fighters were released from Pakistani custody according to a 2006 International Crisis Group report.[18] This was a self-defeating proposition under any circumstances. Moreover, despite the agreement's clear mention of the supremacy of government authority in the area, the militants' flag (al-Rayah) was hoisted at the stadium where the deal was signed. *The News*, a leading English-language newspaper, said in its September 7, 2006, editorial: "[T]he government has all but caved in to the demands of the militants. More ominously, the agreement seems to be a tacit acknowledgment by the government of the growing power and authority of the local Taliban."[19]

Militants upheld their end of the bargain for a few months after the deal was signed, but then returned to their old policies of collaborating with foreign militants and supporting cross-border movement. In the words of a Pakistani writer, these deals in fact provided "much-needed respite to the militants, enabling them to re-group and re-organise themselves."[20] The roughly ten-month-old "peace deal" finally collapsed in July 2007.[21] If anything, militants expanded their support networks during the months of "peace"; even during the relative calm in North Waziristan, militants continued to support some Taliban factions in South Waziristan and parts of Afghanistan.

CONCLUSION

The various accords discussed in this chapter were initially intended to reduce losses for the military, which was ill-equipped and insufficiently motivated to take on militants in Waziristan. The U.S. presence in Afghanistan was highly unpopular from the beginning in the Pashtun areas of both Pakistan and Afghanistan, and going against public opinion in FATA was an uphill task for Pakistan's army. This is often ignored in Western discourse on the subject. In comparison, it is widely recognized that Pakistan all along wanted to remain friendly with at least some Taliban groups that, in time of need, could help it confront the rising Indian influence in Afghanistan. "Peace deals" were in part a product of such factors and fears.

Another relevant issue is Pakistan's efforts at countering Arab and Central Asian fighters and terrorists in the tribal belt. Pakistan achieved many successes in this regard, as compared to its performance against the Pakistani Taliban. In fact, the rise of TTP was a byproduct of Pakistan's campaign against al-Qaeda, as Pakistani militants and extremists in FATA were galvanized and mobilized by Pakistan's military presence and operations. This is why Pakistani security forces often complain that their plight goes unregistered in Western capitals.

Where Pakistan fared poorly was in its failure to understand the true nature of Taliban ideology and emerging radicalization trends in FATA. The Taliban were bound to move into NWFP and beyond if unchecked, and the warnings of many Pakistani writers and journalists went unheeded by the state.[22] To be fair, learning lessons from mistakes is a process, and thus Pakistan's limitations with respect to the 2004 peace deal are understandable. However, once the consequences of that faulty arrangement were exposed in the shape of heightened militancy and expansionist Taliban tendencies, President Musharraf should have adopted tougher and smarter tactics in the FATA.

Perhaps Musharraf's own political ambitions and dependence on approval within the military infrastructure stood in the way. Poor leadership in the NWFP during the 2004-07 timeframe and the dubious policies of the MMA ruling alliance in the province also played an important role in the counterproductive policy choices. Last but not the least, indiscriminate use of force, both by Pakistan and the U.S. (through drone attacks) proved to be a problematic policy in FATA. As an Islambad-based think tank has rightly argued: "A social as well as a political dimension would have to be added to the equation. In absence of a social dimension, the military action might continue endlessly proving extremely detrimental to the state, society, politics and the economy of Pakistan."[13] Pakistan could have been saved a lot of bloodshed if what its army started doing in 2009 in the Swat Valley and South Waziristan, with public and political support, would have begun around 2005.

ENDNOTES

1 *Pashtunwali* is an ancient and chivalrous "code of honor" associated with Pashtuns. It is a social, cultural, and quasi-legal code guiding, governing, and shaping both individual and communal conduct. One of its primary features is *Nanawatay* (Sanctuary): protection given to a person who requests it against his enemies. Any visitor to the area in a difficult situation can ask for sanctuary after telling locals that he means no harm to the people of the area. That person is protected at all costs, and under any circumstances.

2 Tribes that live on both sides of the border include Wazir, Shinwari, Safi, Momund, Salarazai and Mangal.

3 Sartaj Khan, "Changing Pushtun Society," *The News* (Pakistan), Jan. 14, 2010.

4 See Tariq Mahmud Ashraf, "Pakistan's Frontier Corps and the War Against Terrorism—Part Two," *Terrorism Monitor*, Jamestown Foundation, Aug. 11, 2008.

5 See Ismail Khan, "Four Soldiers Die in Wana Attack," *Dawn*, Jan. 10, 2004; Shabana Fayyaz, *Towards a Durable Peace in Afghanistan*, Brief No. 10, Pakistan Security Research Unit, University of Bradford, Apr. 23, 2007.

6 Justin Huggler, "Rebel Tribal Leader is Killed in Pakistan," *Independent* (U.K.), June 19, 2004.

7 Fayyaz, *Towards a Durable Peace in Afghanistan*.

8 Rahimullah Yusufzai, "All Quiet on the North Western Front," *Newsline* (Karachi), May 2004.

9 Ismail Khan & Baqir Sajjad Syed, "Airstrikes Launched in Shakai," *Dawn*, June 12, 2004.

10 Shamim Shahid, "Baitullah, Supporters Lay Down Arms," *The Nation* (Pakistan), Feb. 9, 2005.

11 Author's interview with an official of the FATA Secretariat, Peshawar, July 18, 2009.

12 Amir Mir, "War and Peace in Waziristan," *Asia Times*, May 4, 2005.

13 "Pakistan Pays Tribe al-Qaeda Debt," *BBC News*, Feb. 9, 2005.

14 For Baitullah Mehsud's statement, see Haroon Rashid, "Pakistan Taleban Vow More Violence," *BBC News*, Jan. 29, 2007.

15 Zulfiqar Ghumman, "Taliban Killed 150 Pro-Government Maliks," *Daily Times* (Pakistan), Apr. 18, 2006.

16 For details, see Ismail Khan, "Why the Waziristan Deal is Such a Hard Sell," *Dawn* (Pakistan), Oct. 14, 2006; Muhammad Amir Rana, "Pitfalls in Miramshah

Peace Deal," *Dawn* (Pakistan), Sept. 30, 2006.

17 "Afridi Claims Mullah Omar Backed Waziristan Truce," *The News* (Pakistan), Sept. 28, 2006.

18 "Pakistan's Tribal Areas: Appeasing the Militants," International Crisis Group, Asia Report No. 125, Dec. 11, 2006.

19 Editorial, "Back to Square One?," *The News* (Pakistan), Sept. 7, 2006.

20 Sayed G B Shah Bokhari, "How Peace Deals Help Only Militants," *The News* (Pakistan), July 31, 2008.

21 "Soldier Killed in Pakistan Militant Attack," *Dawn Updates*, July 26, 2007; Haji Mujtiba, "Militants Threaten Attacks in Pakistan's Waziristan," *Reuters*, July 17, 2007; "North Waziristan Clerics to Launch 'Silent Protest,'" *Daily Times* (Pakistan), Aug. 3, 2007.

22 For instance, columnists and writers such as Pervez Hoodbhoy, Rahimullah Yusufzai, Amir Rana, and Ismail Khan regularly projected such scenarios in *Daily Times, The News,* and *Dawn*, three of Pakistan's leading English-language newspapers.

23 "Religious Militancy, Taliban and Peace Deals in FATA," Center for Research and Security Studies, Islamabad, June 16, 2008.

2 Pakistan's Security and the Civil-Military Nexus

by Shuja Nawaz

Pakistan's geostrategic location makes it a critical part of any evaluation of regional security policies, especially reassessments of the situation in Afghanistan. From a Pakistani perspective, any threat analysis must take into account not only the fighting inside Afghanistan but also the major military and economic power to the east: India. Pakistan fears that a hegemonic India would dominate South Asia and bring Pakistan under its thrall. The long-simmering dispute over Kashmir and memories of three major wars with India—including one that led to the breakup of Pakistan and the birth of Bangladesh—still rankle Pakistani minds. The recent Indian elections that returned a stronger Congress Party to power offer some hope of stability in the Indo-Pak relationship, but the weight of history remains heavy.

But today another dangerous conflict is consuming Pakistan, one that may yet become a serious threat to the future of the country as a unified entity. Pakistan faces an internal war against radical Islamists who have established a foothold in the Federally Administered Tribal Areas (FATA), and who have begun to extend their influence and violent activity into the settled areas of the North-West Frontier Province (NWFP) and key parts of the hinterland.

THE PRESENT FIGHT AGAINST ISLAMIST MILITANCY

Suicide bombings and other attacks have been rising dramatically. In 2007, attacks against the military accounted for 47% of suicide attacks, with attacks against the police accounting for another 20%.[1] These have shaken the military establishment.

Pakistan's public overwhelmingly supported a powerful military response, especially against Taliban sympathizers in the Swat and Malakand regions. But operations against the Taliban in the Federally Administered Tribal Areas bordering Afghanistan had been sporadic at best before the invasion of South Waziristan by 30,000 Pakistani army troops late in 2009 that managed to dislocate the headquarters of the Tehrik-e-Taliban Pakistan (the TTP or Pakistani Taliban). Meanwhile the Afghan Taliban, who use the FATA's territory as a sanctuary in their war against the U.S. and its allies in Afghanistan, remain untouched by Pakistani military action. One reason may be political calculation: Pakistan does not wish to anger Pashtun nationalists who may come to power again in Kabul. Beyond that, Pakistan's military lacks the forces and equipment necessary to fight against both its internal Taliban and also the Afghan Taliban—and the military continues to exert great influence over foreign policy relating to both Afghanistan and India.[2]

Indeed, Pakistan's army has dominated the country's political landscape for more than half its life as an independent state. Extended periods of military or quasi-military rule have stunted civilian institutions and inhibited the growth of a free political system. Since the 1950s, Pakistan's army has been at the forefront of foreign policymaking, beginning with a military pact with the United States in 1954.[3] The ensuing military-to-military relationship between the Pentagon and Pakistan's army, despite its ups and downs, has tended to overshadow the civilian relationship between these two on-again, off-again allies. General Pervez Musharraf's turnabout after 9/11, when he threw his support behind the U.S. invasion of Afghanistan against his erstwhile friends the Taliban, was only possible because he was concurrently president and army chief. Pakistan's general public has consistently opposed the U.S. invasion, and the presence of American and foreign forces in Afghanistan. Islamic-leaning groups oppose it on religious grounds, while others regret the blowback effects of a war that has spawned a domestic Taliban movement, strengthened the attraction of al-Qaeda for youth, and fostered a violent insurgency that introduced suicide bombings to Pakistani society.

Pakistan's army, once the most popular national institution, lost its position of respect and dropped in popularity below journalists and lawyers after Musharraf used the threat of the military's coercive power to summarily dismiss the Chief Justice of Pakistan's supreme court in 2007.[4] When this move was overturned by the Supreme Court, Musharraf resorted to a second "coup" by removing the Chief Justice again in November 2007. However, he overestimated his power.

After Musharraf resigned as Chief of Army Staff and appointed General Ashfaq Parvez Kayani in late 2007, he lost his ability to manage Pakistani politics at will. Kayani proved that his primary loyalty was to the army and the country before Musharraf by distancing himself from his former chief and forbidding army officers from meeting all politicians, including Musharraf. The return of former prime ministers Benazir Bhutto and Nawaz Sharif and the subsequent "neutral" position taken by the army in the 2008 elections spelled the end of Musharraf's power. Having lost the army's support, he finally resigned in August 2008. Again, the army's acts of commission and omission were key to that change.

The new army chief, General Kayani, has publicly proclaimed his desire to take the army back to its professional roots. He declared 2008 the Year of the Soldier and 2009 the Year of Training to make up for lost attention to the army's fighting fitness during Musharraf's tenure.[5] He also sought the removal or return of army officers inducted into the civil government and other positions by Musharraf. Some 1200 officers had been parachuted into key slots in ministries, parastatal enterprises, and educational institutions during the Musharraf regime. Kayani also briefed the new civilian government of the Pakistan Peoples Party (PPP) on the country's major security threats and sought its guidance on how to proceed. The army was once against inserted into the battle against insurgents in FATA and the NWFP; unprepared for such warfare, it faced a steep learning curve.

Pakistan's army is a conventional force, poised to defend its eastern borders against India. India makes Pakistan's military nervous not only due to the size of its army (over 1 million strong), but also because of the emergence of a new doctrine called Cold Start that would allow it to move rapidly and without warning into Pakistan.[6] Pakistan's counter-strategy rests on an offensive-defensive approach that involves a massive riposte into India at a point of Pakistan's choosing, enough to seriously hurt the invader. Pakistan's poison-pill defense rests on its nuclear weapons, while India's doctrine eschews first use of its own nuclear weapons.[7] Pakistan had a purposefully ambivalent position on the use of nuclear weapons until November 2008, when President Asif Ali Zardari reportedly also eschewed first use as an option in an interview with an Indian news agency. In the absence of peace or at least an entente with India, Pakistan is constrained to maintain a large conventional force. But the internal insurgency along its western border has caused Pakistan to alter its stance.

Pakistan moved troops into FATA in 2002 after the U.S. promised to reimburse the costs associated with these operations; in 2008, it redeployed the equivalent of six infantry divisions—which comprise its strike force against India—from its eastern border to its western frontier.[8] These forces have been involved in supporting the U.S./NATO effort to seal the western border with Afghanistan against Taliban fighters. They have also been battling insurgents inside Swat, Malakand, and the FATA. In the full-scale assault against militants inside Swat and Malakand in the summer of 2009, the army had some 52,000 troops deployed, moving infantry soldiers from other divisions on the Indian border. In addition, Pakistan deployed a brigade of the Special Services Group, the Pakistani commandos, and nine wings (regiments) of the Frontier Corps.[9] Over 1,300 military deaths and thousands of other casualties proved demoralizing to the army.[10] Moreover, Pakistan's conventional army has had to adapt to unconventional warfare on the fly. It is ill equipped for this war.

The United States has provided financial support to assist Pakistan in covering the costs of moving its forces into FATA, but little effort has been made to give it adequate equipment. There is a lack of modern night-vision devices to monitor the border, and a dearth of helicopters to carry troops rapidly and engage a mobile militant force that strikes across a vast area. Pakistan needs to beef up its forces in the region, but faces a serious problem since it does not have any more forces to spare from the eastern border so long as the Indian threat remains.

Political and economic engagement of the people in FATA, and a clearer national consensus on the nature of the Pakistani state, remain key elements in the fight against militancy inside Pakistan. The responsibility for this rests in civilian hands. It is critical that the civilian government keep the military engaged in discussions on national strategy—so the military plays its role, but does not become the sole instrument of power against militancy. Pakistan must not jeopardize the effectiveness of its military in this process, or it risks losing the one institution that has managed to survive the degradation of Pakistani society under successive periods of autocratic rule.

HISTORICAL INFLUENCES

In order to understand the nexus between Pakistan's army and civil society, one needs to delve into the country's history. Soon after gaining independence in August 1947, Pakistan went to war with India over the Kashmir. Pakistan's fledgling civilian government was still in a chaotic state. Only the military was organized, relatively speaking. Though it took the lead in guiding the military operations, civilian political decision-making was weak and, in the minds of many soldiers, unsatisfactory.

When the war ended in stalemate, a number of disgruntled officers felt that the civilians had "lost" it for Pakistan. A coup was planned but discovered by authorities; a number of officers and civilians were tried and convicted in the Rawalpindi Conspiracy Case in 1951.[11] The army chief at the time, General Muhammad Ayub Khan, was newly installed in his position and felt he had to deal severely with the conspirators.

However, over time Ayub developed a similar view about the inability of civilian leadership to run the country effectively. By 1954, he had already penned a blueprint for a new system of government for Pakistan, with himself at the helm.[12] It took another four years before he overthrew then-President Iskander Mirza in October 1958 and became Chief Martial Law Administrator and President. This solidified the divide between the army and civilians, and laid the foundation for recurrent military interventions.

Ayub's regime lasted over ten years. During that time, he managed to co-opt the civil service and large portions of the pliant political elite. But deep fissures developed between Pakistan's haves and have-nots. Ayub was also unable to manage the noise and disarray of political Pakistan. As a result, when popular protests grew against his rule in 1968 and 1969, he could not withstand the pressure. In an extra-constitutional move, he was persuaded by his favorite army chief General A.M. Yahya Khan to hand power over to Yahya rather than the Speaker of the National Assembly, a Bengali from East Pakistan.[13]

Yahya's ill-fated tenure lasted less than three years, as discontent in East Pakistan led to civil war in that distant province and war with India, resulting in the breakup of Pakistan and the birth of Bangladesh. Yet again, a rigid military system of decision-making did not allow political dialogue to take place concerning the grievances of East Pakistanis against the West Pakistani ruling class. The loss of East Pakistan and military defeat at India's hands temporarily reduced the public's respect for the military, and forced Yahya to resign in December 1971. This allowed a civilian Martial Law Administrator to emerge in the form of Zulfikar Ali Bhutto, the populist leader of the PPP. Bhutto also took over as President, and eventually formulated a new constitution that made him Prime Minister with extraordinary powers; the President was reduced to a figurehead.

It soon became clear that a civilian regime succeeding a military regime would be reluctant to drop most of the powers of its predecessor. Bhutto acquired enormous powers, creating a gap between the center and the periphery, and leading to an insurgency in Balochistan as Bhutto dismissed provincial governments at will and the center took over management of the provinces' natural resources.[14] Political opponents were not allowed to function; private businesses and schools were nationalized in the name of "Islamic socialism."

Gradually the military started asserting itself. The 1977 elections brought the political opposition to the streets to protest what they felt were rigged elections. Bhutto turned to the army to impose order, and there was pushback from the middle ranks. The senior commanders went with Bhutto initially, but when they found their brigadiers and colonels balking at the use of force against civilian protestors, they changed their minds. In July 1977, Bhutto was overthrown by his own handpicked army chief, General Muhammad Zia ul-Haq. History was repeating itself, but with a vengeance. Bhutto was not only removed from power, but over time accused and convicted in a criminal case, and hanged in 1979.

Zia ruled with an iron fist for ten years before dying in an August 1988 airplane crash that has never been satisfactorily investigated. He used his position as Chief of Army Staff to bend the political system to his will, and further exacerbated this manipulation with Islamic rhetoric. In the process, he tried Islamizing the army, thus laying the basis for many of the problems Pakistani society would experience in the decades that followed.[15] The educational system was also Islamized and undermined, as were other major national institutions. Near the end of Zia's tenure, there was some resistance even among the ranks of professional army officers, who resented the fact that the general population was losing respect for the uniform.

Zia also took on the mantle of an Islamic warrior, fighting a jihad against the ungodly Soviet Union in Afghanistan. In the process he helped create the mujahidin (Islamic warriors), and the *madrasas* that would recruit more warriors for that cause. By becoming the conduit for U.S. covert assistance, he made the Inter-Services Intelligence agency (ISI) a major force in Pakistani and regional politics, a position that it maintained into the 21st century.

Zia's successors allowed civilians to re-enter politics, but within limits. Foreign policy on Afghanistan and India, nuclear issues, and defense matters in general remained in the hands of the military. The new army chief, General Mirza Aslam Beg, saw his role as a "referee," even helping gather money from businessmen to pay off politicians; he was especially devoted to fending off the return to politics of Benazir Bhutto, the daughter of the former Prime Minister. The ISI head at the time, Lt. Gen. Hamid Gul, also worked to set up an opposition alliance to Bhutto—and groomed a young Punjabi businessman named Mian Mohammad Nawaz Sharif to take the lead in opposing Bhutto.

The following decade saw repeated changes in government, as Bhutto and Sharif exchanged places twice at the helm as prime minister. Sharif found it difficult to deal with successive army chiefs, including Beg's successor General Asif Nawaz, General Abdul Waheed (who dismissed both Sharif and his opponent President Ghulam Ishaq Khan), and General Jehangir Karamat (whom Sharif forced to resign over a perceived difference of opinion about the creation of a national security council). Sharif picked a relatively junior general, Pervez Musharraf, to head the army in 1998, thinking that his lack of a tribal base in Pakistan would make him more pliable (Musharraf's family came from northern India). But Sharif failed to understand the intrinsic power of the military high command. After Musharraf orchestrated a conflict with India in the frigid wastes of Kargil in northern Kashmir, the army and Sharif were on a collision course. Needless to say, the army had the muscle. When Sharif tried to remove Musharraf from office while the army chief was on an airplane returning from Sri Lanka on October 12, 1999, Musharraf's generals were ready and quickly upended Sharif instead. Pakistan was once more under military rule.

Musharraf's nearly nine-year tenure saw the military enter civilian life in force. Over 1,200 senior military officers were inducted into the administration, educational institutions, and corporations. The U.S. invasion of Afghanistan gave Musharraf a chance to become a much-needed ally of the United States, shades of the Zia era. Politics was stunted and became a directed system under Musharraf's rule, as he unwittingly recreated the patronage networks of the Ayub era. He proved to be an inept politician, and eventually had to make a deal with the exiled Benazir Bhutto to return to Pakistan, with the idea of running the country jointly while keeping Sharif at bay. Bhutto's assassination and the return of Sharif from exile in Jeddah, Saudi Arabia, put an end to Musharraf's scheme. He had to resign in 2008, allowing Bhutto's widower, Asif Ali Zardari, to take the presidency.

The effects of military rule remained, however. Zardari was reluctant to shed the extraordinary powers of his predecessor, and the political system remained in turmoil. A weak coalition of the PPP and an array of opportunistic parties found it difficult to make bold changes in the relationship with the military, and between the Center and provinces in terms of sharing assets and resources. A strong Pakistan Muslim League (Nawaz group) government in the Punjab checkmated it at various junctures. Meanwhile a wary military watched with an eagle eye from the sidelines, stepping out of the shadows every now and then to restore balance in the system without actually entering the political arena. But the betting began on when it might enter the political arena yet again. Watching all this was Pakistan's biggest benefactor and ally, the United States.

THE U.S.-PAKISTAN ROLLER COASTER RELATIONSHIP

Though the United States sees itself as standing for democracy and freedom, it has acted in Pakistan over the decades in a shortsighted manner, making alliances largely with the military to advance its own strategic interests. First, it strengthened the hands of the army by increasing its size and heft in the 1950s via the Baghdad Pact against the Soviets. The U.S. looked the other way as martial law was declared by President Iskander Mirza in October 1958, and then as he was overthrown by Ayub Khan later that month. The U.S. decamped from the scene after the Indo-Pakistan war of 1965, when Pakistan expected the U.S. to assist it. Pakistan then turned to China as its new best friend.

The U.S. returned a decade later, as Yahya Khan played a role in opening the door to China. America sided with Yahya Khan in the 1971 conflict with India, even though he continued his policy of repression in East Pakistan.

During the elder Bhutto's period in power (1971-77), the relationship began to sour because of Pakistan's quest to keep up with India's move toward nuclear weapons, among other reasons. The U.S. kept its distance from Zia ul-Haq and imposed sanctions on Pakistan, isolating it—especially the military—as the U.S. cut its training programs for Pakistani officers. But the Soviet invasion of Afghanistan in December 1979 forced the U.S. to come to terms with Pakistan's dictator in order to use Pakistan's borderland as a staging ground for the covert guerrilla campaign against the Soviet Union in Afghanistan. A decade later, the Soviets exited Afghanistan in ignominious defeat. Soon after General Boris Gromov's 40th Army tanks trundled back into Soviet Uzbekistan on February 15, 1989, the United States packed its bags and left the region. It left in place a "Kalashnikov culture" of political violence and drug running, which had emerged as a major business during the Afghan campaign. Another period of U.S.-Pakistan separation ensued.

Meanwhile Afghanistan fell into civil war and a cycle of destruction that allowed pan-Islamic militancy to emerge. Al-Qaeda found a ready home in Taliban-controlled Afghanistan, and attacked the United States on September 11, 2001. In response, the U.S. attacked Afghanistan and ousted the Taliban. Former American allies, such as Gulbuddin Hekmatyar and Jalaluddin Haqqani, turned against the U.S. following its invasion of Afghanistan. A new phase of the U.S.-Pakistan relationship opened up. Though Musharraf had been a political pariah after his 1999 coup, he suddenly became President George W. Bush's indispensible ally, and assistance began flowing to Pakistan's military to help seal the border with Afghanistan. The United States ignored Pakistan's political system yet again, paying no attention to the demands of Benazir Bhutto and others to pressure Musharraf to restore civilian rule.

Pakistan's entry into the anti-Taliban war spawned a homegrown militant movement in the border region: the Tehrik-e-Taliban Pakistan, or TTP. This militancy entered the North-West Frontier Province, and violence even hit the hinterland. Indeed, TTP leader Baitullah Mehsud was blamed for the assassination of Benazir Bhutto on her return to Pakistan in December 2008.[16] The U.S. government made some amends by eliminating Mehsud in August 2009 via a Predator strike in South Waziristan.[17]

"THE FAULT ... LIES NOT IN OUR STARS...."[18]

The Bard was right. While it is easy for Pakistanis to blame external forces for their woes, and the imbalance between the military and civilians, the fault indeed lies inside Pakistan itself. Shortsighted military and political leaders have found it expedient to use external alliances and purposes to justify military rule, or to allow corrupt governments to continue. Successive civilian governments allowed or helped the military to rise up the ladder of influence in Pakistan.

The Warrant of Precedence, or rank that determines relative seniority in Pakistan's political hierarchy, had placed the military far below civilian ranks at the time of independence.[19] But by elevating the army chief to defense minister in 1954, and then regularly reordering the rank structure, each and every civilian ruler of Pakistan has gradually increased the military's rankings and hence potential power in the overall ruling structure. Interestingly, India retained the old warrant, and Bangladesh reverted back to it during the rule of Prime Minister Khaleda Zia. Pakistan has been moving in the other direction.

The result has been an increasing imbalance in the power structure that will be difficult to dismantle, even if civilian rulers make an effort to do so. A culture of entitlement has been created within the military. The balance between civilians and the military needs to be shifted toward civil supremacy. This must be based on increasing civilian knowledge of the military and its operations; it requires an exhibition of competency by civilian rulers in areas where the military has hitherto played a lead role, such as defense, foreign policy, and nuclear issues.

The economic crisis facing Pakistan also highlights the large drain of resources for defense needs, which consume a substantial portion of its budget. A certain amount of civilian confidence and deftness will be needed to assist the army in changing its orientation from conventional to counter-insurgency warfare, and to reduce its wide economic footprint. Foreign aid to help this transformation will be necessary, since such a change cannot be made overnight and will involve investing in a highly mobile fighting force in place of the current conventional force of 500,000. After an initial spike in spending, defense spending may be able to settle down to lower levels. Further investment will be needed to help retrain demobilized soldiers, and place them in the civilian workforce.

On the external front, civilians need to work with the military to lower tensions with India and ensure that Pakistan's defense remains strong but does not provoke or encourage any external adventures. Pakistan's friends, such as the U.S., Saudi Arabia, and China, can play major roles in this transition by providing Pakistan with a greater sense of security and the economic support for its transition from a military state to a civilian state. A great opportunity exists for the new civilian system to take advantage of the avowed aim of army chief General Kayani to keep the army out of politics. If not, history may repeat itself.

ENDNOTES

1 "Suicide Attacks in Pakistan 2007," *Patronus Analytical, Jan. 15, 2008.*

2 *Editors' note: This chapter was written in late 2009, before such recent events as the arrest in Pakistan of Afghan Taliban leader Mullah Abdul Ghani Baradar. It remains to be seen whether these events signal a broader shift away from the situation that Nawaz describes.*

3 Under this pact Pakistan began receiving military aid from the United States, ostensibly to fight alongside the "free world" against a potential Communist threat from the Soviet Union. In fact, Pakistan viewed its main threat as India, and the army prepared for battle against that rival more than any threat from the north.

4 International Republican Institute, "IRI Index: Pakistan Public Opinion Survey, June 1-15, 2008," slides 34, 38 (accessed Jan. 20, 2010).

5 Ehsan Mehmood Khan, "Kayani Doctrine of Defence Diplomacy," *Pakistan Observer,* Mar. 24, 2009.

6 See Walter C. Ladwig III, "A Cold Start for Hot Wars? The Indian Army's New Limited War Doctrine," *International Security* (Winter 2007/08).

7 Statement by Hamid Ali Rao, Permanent Representative of India to the Conference on Disarmament, First Committee of the 64th Session of the UN General Assembly, Geneva, Oct. 8, 2009.

8 Briefing by Defense Attaché at Pakistani Embassy, Washington, D.C., 2008.

9 Ibid.

10 "Fatalities in Terrorist Violence in Pakistan 2003-2010," South Asia Terrorism Portal (accessed Jan. 20, 2010).

11 See Hasan Zaheer, *The Times and Trials of the Rawalpindi Conspiracy 1951* (Oxford, UK: Oxford University Press, 1998).

12 M. Ayub Khan, *Friends Not Masters* (Oxford, UK: Oxford University Press, 1967), pp. 186-91.

13 Altaf Gauhar, *Ayub Khan: Pakistan's First Military Ruler* (Lahore: Sang-e-Meel Publications, 1993).

14 For further discussion, see Selig Harrison, *In Afghanistan's Shadow: Baluch Nationalism and Soviet Temptations* (Washington, DC: Carnegie Endowment for International Peace, 1981).

15 For more on how shifts in Pakistan's military contributed to the country's problems with Islamic militancy, see Daveed Gartenstein-Ross's chapter in this volume.

16 "Bhutto Killing Blamed on al-Qaeda," *BBC News,* Dec. 28, 2007.

17 See Bill Roggio, "Baitullah Mehsud Dead; Hakeemullah New Leader of Pakistani Taliban," *Long War Journal,* Aug. 25, 2009.

18 William Shakespeare, *The Tragedy of Julius Caesar,* act 1, scene 2.

19 Shuja Nawaz, *Crossed Swords: Pakistan, its Army, and the Wars Within* (Oxford, UK: Oxford University Press, 2008), p. xxxix.

3 | Religious Militancy in Pakistan's Military and Inter-Services Intelligence Agency

by Daveed Gartenstein-Ross

A deadly suicide bombing hit India's embassy in Kabul on July 7, 2008. After the U.S. learned that the attack seemingly implicated elements of Pakistan's powerful Inter-Services Intelligence agency (ISI), American planners decided that the U.S. needed to deliver a stern warning to Pakistan. Late in the month, CIA deputy director Stephen R. Kappes traveled to Islamabad to present Pakistani officials with information about the ISI's ties to extremists in the country's tribal areas. The *New York Times* opined that this was "the bluntest American warning to Pakistan since shortly after the Sept. 11 attacks about the ties between the spy service and Islamic militants."[1]

Pakistan is, of course, critical to the U.S.'s present efforts in South Asia. After the October 2001 U.S. invasion of Afghanistan toppled the Taliban, most of al-Qaeda's senior leadership relocated to Pakistan's Federally Administered Tribal Areas, the mountainous region that borders Afghanistan. Once there, the terrorists set about finding allies within tribal society. Though Pakistan's military mounted a campaign to flush out al-Qaeda after the group was connected to assassination attempts against Pervez Musharraf, the military suffered so many losses that Musharraf eventually concluded he had no option but to negotiate with his would-be killers. In March and September 2006 he consummated both halves of the Waziristan accords; subsequent "peace deals" followed that have similarly helped al-Qaeda establish a new safe haven in Pakistan.[2]

American analysts increasingly believe that support for religious militancy within Pakistan's military and ISI is one of the key obstacles to formulating a sound approach toward the region: as President Obama remarked in his December 2009 West Point address, "success in Afghanistan is inextricably linked to our partnership with Pakistan."[3] It is important that policymakers and scholars understand how support for religious militancy has gained a foothold in these institutions, and the problems that it now poses.

THE ORIGINS OF PAKISTAN'S MILITARY AND ISI

Pakistan's military and intelligence services were originally shaped by the country's colonial experience. The ISI was formed by a British army officer, Major General R. Cawthome, in 1948. The agency was charged with coordinating the intelligence functions of Pakistan's army, navy, and air force.

Shuja Nawaz notes that Pakistan's army had an elitist orientation at the outset. "The senior echelons were still British officers who had opted to stay on," he writes, "and they were in turn succeeded by their native clones, men who saw the army as a unique institution, separate and apart from the rest of civil society and authority."[4] Though some commentators believe that the seeds of the army's later Islamization were planted from its very inception,[5] it is clear that there was significant tension early in the relationship between Pakistan's military and its Islamic parties. For example, General Mohammad Ayub Khan, Pakistan's first military ruler, wrote in his diary in 1967 that "[t]he mullah regards the educated Muslims as his deadliest enemy and the rival for power," and that "we have got to take on all those [mullahs] who are political mischief-makers."[6]

Zulfikar Ali Bhutto, whose period in power ran from 1971-1977, broadened the ISI by creating an internal wing. He was concerned with bolstering his own political power, and his personal leadership had a paranoid strand. Bhutto asked the ISI to conduct surveillance on friend and foe alike, and the agency kept dossiers on a wide range of figures. Ironically, the internal wing that Bhutto established later played a role in the military coup that toppled him in July 1977. That coup brought to power General Muhammad Zia ul-Haq, who consciously pushed Pakistani society in a more religious direction, and concentrated his efforts on the military in particular.

MUHAMMAD ZIA UL-HAQ'S ISLAMIZATION POLICIES

The fact that Zia embarked on an ambitious plan for Islamizing Pakistan is well known. But observers often overlook two aspects of Zia's changes. One is that Islamization had clearly begun before Zia took office, and thus cannot be ascribed solely to "the inadvertent outcome of decisions by some governments."[7] The second is the breadth of religious policies implemented during these years, particularly those designed to regulate the military, and the impact these policies had on the organizational culture of Pakistan's army.

Stephen P. Cohen of the Brookings Institution points out that the army began Islamizing under Bhutto. "Zulfikar himself ordered alcohol removed from the mess," Cohen says, "and one of the reasons that he picked Zia as the army's chief of staff may have been that Zia was seen as a pious general."[8] Though Bhutto was secular in outlook, Islamists were politically ascendant at the time, and these gestures were designed to placate them.

After the coup that removed Bhutto, Zia served as prime minister for around ten years, the longest tenure of any Pakistani executive. He had been involved from an early age with the Tablighi Jamaat, a socially conservative grassroots Islamic movement. Zia had served in the Royal Indian Army prior to Pakistan's creation, and his religiosity was apparent during his military service: he once explained that while other officers' free time was occupied by drinking, gambling, and dancing, he spent his in prayer.

Zia's background and religious zeal translated into his government's adoption of overtly Muslim public policy positions, and its imposition of Islamic norms and customs. These changes began almost immediately; one observer, writing less than six months after Zia took power, noted that a "general Islamic tone pervades everything." He continued:

> A state enterprise advertises for a manager "who should be a God fearing and practicing Muslim." Floggings are common. Television has been greatly changed—to the accompaniment of public protest in the letters-to-the-editors column of the newspapers. Total closure of eating and drinking places between sunup and sunset marked Ramzan, the holy month of fasting, and no tea was served in business establishments or offices, private or public.... Islamic laws on theft, drinking, adultery, and the protection of freedom of belief are to be enforced from [February 1979].[9]

Zia's government created *sharia* courts to determine the religious legitimacy of all laws, and invalidate those they deemed improper. The government simultaneously tried to create an interest-free "Islamic economy."

Zia devoted particular attention to changing the culture of Pakistan's military. His reforms went beyond Bhutto's nascent changes in three major ways. First, the military's training came to include Islamic teachings. Officers, for example, were required to read S.K. Malik's *The Qur'anic Concept of War*, and a Directorate of Religious Instruction oversaw the Islamic education of the officer corps. Second, religious criteria were incorporated into officers' promotion requirements and promotion exams. Many skilled officers with secular outlooks were passed over for promotion while religious conservatives reached top levels of command. Third, Zia reinforced these policies by mandating formal obedience to Islamic rules within the military. He required not only that soldiers attend Friday congregational prayers at regimental mosques, but also that units bring mullahs with them to the front lines of combat.

At the same time that Zia implemented these policies, the demographics of the officer corps naturally shifted. The first generation of officers from the country's social elites was being replaced by new junior officers from Pakistan's poorer northern districts. Zahid Hussain notes that "[t]he spirit of liberalism, common in the 'old' army, was practically unknown to them. They were products of a social class that, by its very nature, was conservative and easily influenced by Islamic fundamentalism."[10]

Zia's policies, coupled with the demographic shift in the junior officer corps, moved the military in a more religious, and more fundamentalist, direction. But this shift was significantly accelerated by external circumstances. Soon after Zia came to power, the Soviet Union invaded Afghanistan on behalf of a pro-Soviet regime that was threatened by Islamic rebels. The fateful invasion not only imposed great costs on the Soviet Union that contributed to its collapse, but also spurred Pakistan and the U.S. to support anti-Soviet mujahidin. The ISI grew exponentially during this period, as did relationships between the Pakistani military and Islamic militants.

THE ISI, THE AFGHAN-SOVIET WAR, AND THE TALIBAN

Though the Soviets hoped their 1979 invasion would quickly secure the country for their proxy government, they became embroiled in a draining conflict. The ISI was critical to anti-Soviet efforts, funneling weapons and money to the mujahidin and training them. In doing so, the ISI benefited from significant foreign support: the CIA's funding of the anti-Soviet resistance reached about $500 million per year at its height, money that was doubled by Saudi Arabia's decision to match U.S. funding dollar for dollar.

The relationship between the CIA and ISI developed on the ISI's terms, with Zia minimizing contact between the Americans and the Afghan mujahidin. This arrangement offered the U.S. plausible deniability while giving Pakistan access to a large amount of American money, and allowing Pakistani officials to forge their own relationships with the Afghans.

Though there were a range of mujahidin factions, the ISI preferred to fund Islamic fundamentalists and ethnic separatists. The major reason for this was strategic: the ISI perceived Islamists as fearless fighters, and thought they could more easily be transformed into a Pakistani proxy. But there was also an ideological dimension: many of Pakistan's officers had come to sympathize with, or even adopt, a hardline religious outlook. As funding for the mujahidin grew, so did the ISI. By the time the war ended, it had mushroomed from a staff of around 2,000 to 40,000 employees and a $1 billion budget.

After the Soviet retreat, little united the disparate mujahidin factions other than their common fight against the Soviet-backed regime of Mohammad Najibullah. It is thus unsurprising that the country fell into civil war in 1992, after the mujahidin captured the capital of Kabul. (The utterly foreseeable nature of Afghanistan's collapse is one of the reasons that the U.S.'s refusal to continue its engagement in the country following the USSR's withdrawal is rightly regarded as a major foreign policy failure.) Ahmed Rashid considers it significant that Kabul fell not to the Pashtun mujahidin factions, but rather to the better-organized Tajik forces. "It was a devastating psychological blow because for the first time in 300 years the Pashtuns had lost control of the capital," he writes in his definitive book on the Taliban. "An internal civil war began almost immediately."[11] The ISI remained involved as various warlords and former mujahidin vied for power.

During the Afghan-Soviet war, a network of *madrasas* funded by Saudi Arabia had sprung up near Pakistan's border with Afghanistan. Among other things, these schools served a strategic purpose: students were indoctrinated with a militant religious ideology designed to make them more fervent fighters. This network of schools ultimately gave birth to the Taliban. There are a number of accounts of how the group formed in 1994, but Rashid finds one story to be the most credible. In this telling, two neighbors informed

Mullah Mohammed Omar that a warlord "had abducted two teenage girls, their heads had been shaved and they had been taken to a military camp and repeatedly raped." In response, Omar and thirty talibs "attacked the base, freeing the girls and hanging the commander from the barrel of a tank."[12]

Mullah Omar was born into a Pashtun tribe in 1959. As a young man, "he moved to Singesar village in the Mewand district of Kandahar province, where he became the village mullah and opened a small *madrassa*."[13] Omar was wounded four times in the fighting that gripped the country following the Soviet invasion: the most notable injury was the permanent blinding of his right eye.

The Taliban's power grew rapidly in Afghanistan for a variety of reasons, including the fact that they were effective fighters and enjoyed significant sponsorship from the ISI. "The ISI helped the Taliban take the key cities of Jalalabad and the capital Kabul," the *Christian Science Monitor* notes, "and continued to back them as they secured about 95 percent of Afghanistan."[14] As the Taliban expanded, it implemented a harsh version of Islamic law.

The Taliban offered Osama bin Laden and his followers safe haven after they were forced to flee Sudan. Al-Qaeda established a network of training camps, and ISI agents formed relationships with the terrorist group. The *New York Times* has reported that the ISI "even used Al Qaeda camps in Afghanistan to train covert operatives for use in a war of terror against India."[15] The ISI's use of al-Qaeda camps to train fighters destined for Kashmir was revealed in August 1998, after the U.S. struck camps near Khost, Afghanistan, in retaliation for the bombing of U.S. embassies in Kenya and Tanzania. "The casualties included several members of a Kashmiri militant group supported by Pakistan who were believed to be training in the Qaeda camps," the *Times* stated.[16]

As with the ISI's preference for supporting religious extremist anti-Soviet fighters, there were both strategic and ideological reasons for sponsoring the Taliban. The strategic reason was that the government in Kabul had historically been hostile to Pakistan, and Pakistani strategic planners thought the Taliban could serve as a proxy providing them with "strategic depth." But the ideological reasons behind the ISI's support for the Taliban were also growing.

SUPPORT FOR MILITANCY IN KASHMIR

The revelation that the ISI used al-Qaeda camps to train fighters destined for the disputed state of Jammu and Kashmir (generally known simply as Kashmir) touches on a second conflict in which Pakistan used religious militants to advance their strategic ends.

The conflict over Kashmir has its origins in the partition of India and Pakistan. Under British rule, 562 different princely states "had retained varying degrees of administrative independence through treaties with Britain concluded during the process of colonial penetration."[17] Kashmir's ruler, Maharajah Hari Singh, wanted his state to remain independent even though a segment of his Muslim-majority citizenry wanted to join Pakistan. Pakistanis felt cheated when the Boundary Commission led by Sir Cyril Radcliffe gave India two Muslim-majority subdivisions in Gurdaspur district; the resulting land access to Kashmir left India with a legitimate claim to the princely state.

Pakistan's disorganized government responded with a strategy of unconventional warfare that relied on hastily-trained Pashtun tribesmen. Husain Haqqani notes that precious little thought went into these plans. The assumption "was that the Kashmiri people would support the invading tribal *lashkar*," he writes, with no consideration of "the prospect of failure or to what might happen if the Indian army got involved in forestalling a Pakistani *fait accompli* against the Kashmiri maharajah."[18] Seeking military help from India, Maharajah Hari Singh signed accession papers, the legitimacy of which Pakistan continues to dispute.

This was the origin of the 1947-48 war between India and Pakistan, and Kashmir has been a source of tension ever since. India and Pakistan fought over Kashmir again in 1965, but the mujahidin's success in the Afghan-Soviet conflict made Pakistani planners think they could use unconventional warfare more capably than they had in 1947. This renewed warfare through proxies began on July 31, 1988, when a number of explosions rocked Kashmir's capital Srinagar. Though the bombings were claimed by the Jammu and Kashmir Liberation Front (JKLF), Owen Bennett Jones explains that the ISI had a hand in them. "The JKLF agreed to recruit would-be militants in Indian-held Kashmir, bring them across the line of control and deliver them to ISI trainers," he writes. "The ISI in turn agreed to provide the JKLF fighters with weapons and military instruction."[19]

The Kashmir insurgency escalated following the Soviet Union's departure from Afghanistan. Pakistan's population flooded with unemployed mujahidin, and sectarian violence increased.[20] The ISI's solution was to send the mujahidin to Kashmir. Just as ISI officers developed important relationships with militants during the Afghan-Soviet war, they did so also during the Kashmir conflict.

The ISI initially relied on the JKLF to lead the insurgency, but soon other ISI-supported jihadist groups began to operate in Kashmir as well. As of 2001,

India's Research and Analysis Wing estimated that "annual ISI expenditure to the main militant organisations runs to between US$125 and $250 million a year."[21] The U.S. now considers a number of groups that the ISI supported in Kashmir to be strategic threats because they have extended the reach of their terrorist activities beyond Kashmir, and have developed working relationships with al-Qaeda.

One such group is Lashkar-e-Taiba (LeT), the first jihadist group to introduce suicide bombings to Kashmir, which was founded in 1990 as an outgrowth of Markaz Dawat-ul-Irshad. India blamed LeT for the attack on its parliament in December 2001, and the group has subsequently been implicated in both the 2006 commuter rail bombings in Mumbai and the infamous November 2008 "urban warfare" attack in the same city. Another group that falls into this category is Jaish-e-Mohammed (JeM), which has declared war against the U.S. JeM has been accused of playing a role in the 2001 Indian parliament attack, and Pakistan's government has "implicated JEM for ... two assassination attempts on former Pakistani President Pervez Musharraf."[22]

A Council on Foreign Relations backgrounder outlines some of the links between Kashmiri militant groups and al-Qaeda:

> Many terrorists active in Kashmir received training in the same *madrasas*, or Muslim seminaries, where Taliban and al-Qaeda fighters studied, and some received military training at camps in Taliban-ruled Afghanistan. Leaders of some of these terror groups also have al-Qaeda connections. The long-time leader of the Harakat ul-Mujahideen group, Fazlur Rehman Khalil, signed al-Qaeda's 1998 declaration of holy war, which called on Muslims to attack all Americans and their allies. Maulana Masood Azhar, who founded the Jaish-e-Mohammed organization, traveled to Afghanistan several times to meet Osama bin Laden. Azhar's group is suspected of receiving funding from al-Qaeda, U.S. and Indian officials say.[23]

During the 1990s, the ISI also supported stateless militancy outside the region. For example, it backed militants in Bosnia and Herzegovina.[24] Thus, by the time of the 9/11 attacks, Pakistan had an entrenched policy of supporting these groups. Though Musharraf altered the country's course after U.S. deputy secretary of state Richard Armitage's famous threat to bomb Pakistan "back to the Stone Age,"[25] Pakistan has never entirely abandoned its institutional support for Islamic militancy.

THE 9/11 ATTACKS AND THEIR AFTERMATH

On January 12, 2002, Musharraf announced Pakistan's dramatic about-face, declaring that no group based in Pakistan "would be allowed to indulge in terrorism in the name of religion."[26] He banned five jihadist groups that day, including LeT and JeM, and also sacked pro-Taliban commanders at the top levels of the ISI and military. Altogether, Musharraf "forced the reassignment or resignation of Pakistan's intelligence chief, two top generals and a number of other military commanders—most of whom were regarded as pro-Taliban or Islamist."[27] The fired commanders included ISI chief Lt.-Gen. Mahmood Ahmed and corps commander Lt.-Gen. Mohammed Aziz Khan.

Mahmood was in fact representative of many problems within the ISI. Pakistan dispatched him to Kandahar in September 2001, after al-Qeada's attacks on the U.S., to try to convince Mullah Omar to surrender Osama bin Laden. After meeting with Mullah Omar alone, Mahmood sent a delegation of Islamic scholars to speak with him. Zahid Hussain notes that this move was clearly not intended to persuade Mullah Omar:

> [T]he delegation comprised hardline pro-Taliban clerics headed by Mufti Nizamuddin Shamzai, who later issued a *fatwa* (religious edict) for jihad against the American-led coalition forces. While he himself led violent protests against the Musharraf government, one of his sons went to Afghanistan to fight on behalf of the Taliban. There was a strong suspicion that the ISI chief may have been involved in deception. Some officials suggest that he had told Mullah Omar to remain steadfast and not succumb to American pressure.[28]

In addition to the firings, Musharraf made other changes aimed at purging officers with extremist sympathies. In February 2002, for example, Pakistan began "to disband two major units of its powerful intelligence service that had close links to Islamic militants in Afghanistan and Kashmir."[29] But many military and ISI officers remained tied to the mujahidin with whom they had built relations over the course of two decades.

Today, the breadth and depth of the Pakistani military and ISI's support for Islamic militancy is shrouded by secrecy, denials, and a lack of publicly-available information. There is broad agreement among informed analysts that support for jihadist groups occurs at three levels within Pakistan's ISI and military, although there is no agreement about how representative each of these categories is.

First, there is an institutional policy of support within the ISI for actors such as the Haqqani network, Mullah Omar's Taliban, and perhaps other jihadist groups that are closely aligned with al-Qaeda.

Second, beyond the ISI's explicit policies, rogue elements of Pakistan's ISI and military have supported jihadist attacks. These elements have been implicated in several recent incidents, including the November 2008 Mumbai attacks, the September 2008 Islamabad Marriott bombing, the July 2008 bombing of India's embassy in Kabul, and assassination attempts directed at Pervez Musharraf and Benazir Bhutto. These may, in fact, only be the tip of the iceberg. There are several unanswered questions about these rogue factions. One is whether the rogue elements are acting individually, or if they constitute factions within the ISI and the military. A second question is whether some of the incidents attributed to rogue factions in fact represent official ISI policies. Both Pakistan and the U.S. have incentives to categorize the ISI's sponsorship of major terrorist acts as the work of rogues even if this is not in fact the case: Pakistan to avoid major international confrontations (particularly with India), and the U.S. to perhaps conceal the depth of the conundrum it faces with its strategic partner in South Asia.

Third, retired ISI and military officers with connections to Islamic militancy often remain influential following their retirement. One example is former ISI head Hamid Gul, who in 2003 declared that "God will destroy the United States in Iraq and Afghanistan and wherever it will try to go from there." In late 2008, the U.S. sent a secret document to Pakistan's government linking Gul to the Taliban and al-Qaeda, and India has demanded his arrest in connection with the November 2008 Mumbai terrorist attacks.[30]

There is frequently overlap between these three levels. For example, retired ISI officers often work for the organization as contractors, and a number of Western analysts believe that contractors are the "weakest link" insofar as support for jihadist groups against the express policies of the ISI is concerned.

CONCLUSION

It is clear that all three levels of support for religious militancy within Pakistan's military and ISI create problems for U.S. interests in the region. For example, some strategists are concerned that attempts to better coordinate U.S. airpower with Pakistani ground forces—which is frequently advocated on the Pakistani side—will result in military plans being leaked to the militants whom they target.

One of the U.S.'s overarching goals in its diplomacy with Pakistan should be to persuade Pakistan's government to cease support for jihadist groups where there is an institutional policy of doing so. Moreover, as Zahid Hussain has observed, when Musharraf allied with the U.S. after 9/11 he was "taking Pakistan to war with itself."[31] In other words, these problems come not just from continuing official support for religious militancy, but also from an institutional culture and outlook that grew over decades. The road to reversing this course will not be easy, but clearly understanding the problem—and acting upon it—is necessary.

ENDNOTES

1   Mark Mazzetti & Eric Schmitt, "C.I.A. Outlines Pakistan Links with Militants," *New York Times*, July 30, 2008.

2   See Hassan Abbas's contribution to this volume, which comprehensively examines the Waziristan peace deals.

3   President Barack Obama, "Remarks by the President in Address to the Nation on the Way Forward in Afghanistan and Pakistan," West Point, N.Y., Dec. 1, 2009.

4   Shuja Nawaz, *Crossed Swords: Pakistan, Its Army, and the Wars Within* (Oxford: Oxford University Press, 2008), p. xxxi.

5   See, e.g., Husain Haqqani, *Pakistan: Between Mosque and Military* (Washington, DC: Carnegie Endowment for International Peace, 2005), p. 29.

6   *Diaries of Field Marshal Mohammad Ayub Khan 1966-1972* (Karachi: Oxford University Press, Craig Baxter ed., 2007), p. 49.

7   Haqqani, *Pakistan: Between Mosque and Military*, p. 2.

8   Author telephone interview with Stephen P. Cohen, Nov. 24, 2008.

9   W. Eric Gustafson, "Pakistan 1978: At the Brink Again?," *Asian Survey*, Feb. 1979, pp. 161-62.

10   Zahid Hussain, *Frontline Pakistan: The Struggle with Militant Islam* (New York: Columbia University Press, 2007), p. 20.

11   Ahmed Rashid, *Taliban: Militant Islam, Oil and Fundamentalism in Central Asia* (New Haven, CT: Yale University Press, 2000), p. 21.

12   Ibid., p. 25.

13   Ibid., p. 24.

14   Robert Marquand & Scott Baldauf, "Will Spies Who Know Tell the U.S.?," *Christian Science Monitor*, Oct. 3, 2001.

15   James Risen & Judith Miller, "Pakistani Intelligence Had Links to al Qaeda, U.S. Officials Say," *New York Times*, Oct. 29, 2001.

16   Ibid.

17   Haqqani, *Pakistan: Between Mosque and Military*, p. 27.

18 Ibid., p. 28.

19 Owen Bennett Jones, *Pakistan: Eye of the Storm* (New Haven, CT: Yale University Press, 2003), pp. 82-83.

20 Hassan Abbas, *Pakistan's Drift into Extremism: Allah, the Army, and America's War on Terror* (Armonk, NY: M.E. Sharpe, 2005), pp. 12-13.

21 Peter Chalk, "Pakistan's Role in the Kashmir Insurgency," *Jane's Intelligence Review*, Sept. 1, 2001.

22 Jamal Afridi, "Kashmir Militant Extremists," *Council on Foreign Relations Backgrounder*, July 9, 2009.

23 Ibid.

24 Haqqani, *Pakistan: Between Mosque and Military*, p. 292.

25 Pervez Musharraf, *In the Line of Fire: A Memoir* (New York: Free Press, 2006), p. 201.

26 Hussain, *Frontline Pakistan*, p. 51.

27 Refet Kaplan, "Pakistani President Purges Pro-Taliban Military Leaders," *FoxNews.com*, Oct. 8, 2001.

28 Hussain, *Frontline Pakistan*, p. 43.

29 Douglas Jehl, "Pakistan to Cut Islamists' Links to Spy Agency," *New York Times*, Feb. 20, 2002.

30 See Ansar Abbasi, "Secret Document Confirms Hameed Gul Wanted by the US," *International News* (Pakistan), Dec. 7, 2008 (describing secret U.S. document); Emily Wax & Rama Lakshmi, "Indian Official Points to Pakistan," *Washington Post*, Dec. 6, 2008 (describing the Indian demand for Gul's arrest).

31 Hussain, *Frontline Pakistan*, p. viii.

4

Pakistan's Islamist Frontier: Islamic Politics and U.S. Policy in Pakistan's North-West Frontier

by Joshua T. White

Pakistan's North-West Frontier Province (NWFP) is increasingly a geographic and ideological focal point for "religious" extremism. Bordering Afghanistan and the troubled Federally Administered Tribal Areas (FATA), the NWFP has experienced a social and political shift over the past two decades toward conservative, and sometimes militant, Islam. The overwhelming success of the Muttahida Majlis-e-Amal (MMA) Islamist alliance in the 2002 NWFP provincial elections—an alliance dominated by conservative leaders who espoused anti-American rhetoric and shared an ideological affinity with the Taliban—appeared to many to signal a shift toward a "Talibanized" Frontier inimical to both Pakistani and U.S. interests.[1]

That narrative, however, turned out to be too simple. Rather than acting in the mold of the Afghan Taliban, the MMA bent to the exigencies of governance and moderated on a host of policies. Rather than forging a qualitatively new political form in the Frontier, the Islamist alliance succumbed to the cyclical nature of local politics, losing spectacularly to Pashtun nationalist parties in the 2008 general elections. And rather than maintaining their hold on right-of-center religious politics, MMA constituent parties were outflanked by a new class of "religious" actors operating on the blurred boundary between formal politics and insurgent militancy.

How dramatically has the Frontier changed? In 2002, the preeminent concern of policymakers was that a coalition of anti-American and pro-*sharia* religious parties would establish an electoral foothold, and use their political position to enact an array of discriminatory laws in the mold of the Afghan Taliban. Now, the preoccupations of policymakers are more profound and more complex. Today the concerns—to list only a few—are that al-Qaeda has reconstituted its operations in the FATA; that regional strongmen are facilitating cross-border militancy against coalition forces in Afghanistan; that local Taliban-like insurgencies are gaining ground in the settled areas of the NWFP; and that religious parties, once feared as the vanguard of Talibanization, are now losing the ability to draw religiously-minded young people away from insurgent activity and into the political mainstream.[2]

In light of these changes, the key objective of this chapter is to examine through a political lens the rise and fall of the MMA, and the concomitant rise of new insurgent actors. This objective is important because much of the analysis of religious politics in the Frontier focuses on militant capabilities and outcomes rather than political and social drivers (objectives, rivalries, partnerships, leverage, etc.). In doing so, it is easy to miss the fundamentally political nature of the conflicts in today's Frontier. In 2002, for example, observers often made the mistake of reading the MMA through the lens of the Afghan Taliban; in doing so they underestimated the degree to which the Pakistani Islamists would be shaped by local political interests. Similarly, observers today often make the mistake of reading the new class of neo-Taliban insurgent groups narrowly through the lens of al-Qaeda and the Waziri militant networks; in doing so they again underestimate the ways in which these insurgents and their agendas are woven deeply into the fabric of both local and regional politics.

THE RISE AND SCOPE OF ISLAMIC POLITICAL INFLUENCE

The history of Islamist influence in the Pakistani political process has been extensively documented. As the focus of this chapter is on the changing dynamics of political Islam, the narrative herein focuses on the origins and development of Pakistan's major Islamist parties, their interaction with the state and external actors, and the politics which lie behind their agitation. This history is essential for framing a proper evaluation of the post-2001 Frontier, in which the religious parties—and their insurgent affiliates—played a central role in reshaping the region's political and security environment.

Pre-1947: Religio-political movements. The ninety years between the failed uprising of 1857 and the partition of 1947 laid the groundwork for Islamic political expression in independent Pakistan. The history of this period is multifaceted and deeply complex, and has received excellent scholarly treatment in several recent works.[3] A number of important movements arose during this period, particularly in the North-West Frontier Province and the Indo-Afghan borderlands.

The first of these was the uprising of 1858, which arose in the areas dominated by the Yusufzai clan—the region now roughly constituting the districts Buner, Malakand, Mardan, Swabi, and Swat. This region has a centuries-long history of alliances-of-convenience between charismatic spiritual leaders and their tribal supporters. What began as an internecine struggle between two such power blocs eventually coalesced into overt opposition to the British.[4] Akhund Abdul Ghaffur, a Sufi *pir* (saint), cultivated a network of mujahidin who were known to the British as the "Hindustani Fanatics," as well as a line of *murids* (disciples) who would come to have enormous influence in the religious and political development of the adjacent tribal areas.[5] A confrontation unfolded in 1863 between these mujahidin and the British, and following a pattern which would continue well into the modern era, the conflict was eventually resolved along essentially political lines. The Akhund, fearful of the prospect of British armies advancing into an area which had resisted foreign rule for nearly 300 years, turned on his allies and assisted the British in expelling the mujahidin. By assisting the British, he assured his own continued role in the northern frontier areas, and at the same time leveraged British action to decapitate his leading religio-political rival.

The three decades which followed the Swat uprising were by no means uneventful for British administrators on the frontier. What looked to the British like a simple plan of rationalizing a once-chaotic frontier policy looked to the tribesmen like a scheme designed to encircle, co-opt, and control regions which had for centuries remained autonomous. As a result, the tribes rose up in 1897, first in Malakand, and then throughout nearly all the frontier regions. The resistance of 1897 did not last long in the face of large-scale British military operations.

The creation of the NWFP as a formal political space in 1901 not only influenced the ways in which the British conceived of their project of frontier governance, but also began to influence local conceptions of ethnic Pashtun identity. Important changes in mass politics were also taking shape in the Frontier.

Muslims launched the Khilafat movement in 1919, which agitated against the proposed abolition of the Ottoman caliphate. One of the stranger sub-narratives of the Khilafat story was the attempted *hijrat* (migration) of tens of thousands of Muslims from India into Afghanistan in 1920, seeking to cross the Durand Line into the *dar al-Islam* (abode of Islam). While both the Khilafat movement and the *hijrat* were failures, these movements marked the first attempt to mobilize pan-Islamic sentiment across the subcontinent, and presented the religious clerics of the Frontier an opportunity to rally the Pashtun in opposition to the British, build networks, and try their hand at activist politics.

The locus of Islamic agitation in the Frontier shifted somewhat in the 1930s and '40s, away from Swat, the Peshawar valley, and Afghanistan proper, and toward the tribal agencies. In 1930, the government mobilized its largest frontier operations since the war of 1919, in response to *lashkars* raised by local mullahs and Khilafat committees. The British were also forced to confront quite regularly the specter of *ad hoc* tribal militias led by charismatic leaders in Waziristan. Often these leaders used pan-Islamic language to provide a veneer of legitimacy for their project of aggregating self-interested tribal factions.

Pre-1947: The emergence of Islamist parties. The two major Islamic political movements operating in Pakistan today both have their antecedents in pre-1947 India. The first of these are the Deobandis. This movement traces its roots to modern-day Uttar Pradesh, where a group of clerics founded the Dar ul-Ulum Deoband in 1866. Established in the wake of the failed uprising in 1857, this *madrasa* became the focal point of a wider religious revivalist movement which sought to reconsolidate and refocus the religious and cultural life of the Muslim *ummah* on the subcontinent. Far from being political, the early Deobandis were for the most part "inward-looking and primarily concerned with the Islamic quality of individual lives."[6]

Through the First World War, most Deobandi clerics remained apolitical. Some, however, came to believe that the revivalist message which began at Deoband had to be broadened to include a political restoration of the Muslim community. Some of these clerics entered the political realm. A great number eventually formalized their political participation by joining the Jamiat Ulema-e-Hind (Assembly of Indian Clerics, JUH), a party established in 1919.

Throughout the 1920s, JUH clerics struggled to define their political agenda. The party's activist energy, however, could not be sustained after the failure of the Khilafat movement, and from the end of the 1920s to the middle of the 1940s, the JUH again turned inward. But by the mid-1940s, the majority of Deobandi *ulema* were no longer debating whether or not they ought to engage in politics; the question before them was, "politics toward what end?" While they shared an opposition to British rule, deep fault lines began to emerge surrounding the "two-nation theory" proposed by Muhammad Ali Jinnah and the Muslim League, and its call for Pakistan as a homeland for Muslims of the Indian subcontinent. In 1945, the JUH split over this issue: the pro-Muslim League faction became the Jamiat Ulema-e-Islam (JUI), and the JUH maintained its affiliation with the Indian National Congress Party, arguing that the creation of Pakistan would divide and weaken the Muslims of India.[7]

The JUI performed poorly in the 1946 NWFP elections. In 1947 India was partitioned, and NWFP joined the new Pakistani state. In spite of competition between the JUH and the JUI, neither side was able to gain overwhelming support among the Muslims living in the frontier areas. There was a wide diversity of opinion among the Pashtuns as to whether the establishment of Pakistan was in their interest, and if it was, whether Jinnah and the Muslim League represented legitimate Islamic principles. The JUI began in the new state with limited influence in the Frontier, but would in time emerge as one of Pakistan's leading Islamist movements.

The second important movement to emerge out of the pre-Partition milieu was the Jamaat-e-Islami (JI). The Jamaat, as it is known, was founded by Deobandi cleric Maulana Abul A'la Maududi in 1941. Unlike the JUI, which drew largely from a rural support base and recruited the clerical classes, the JI sought to recruit technocrats and activists, and drew its support predominantly from the "devout middle classes" of Pakistan's urban centers.[8] Opposed to the Muslim League, the JI was Maududi's attempt to institutionalize a movement of Islamic renewal. The Jamaat's Islamist vision was somewhat different from that of the Deobandi clerical class. Maududi's ideology emphasized the importance of reforming the state and the legal apparatus, and his focus on political transformation influenced the writings of Arab Islamist intellectuals such as Hassan al-Banna and Sayyid Qutb. This ideological bias toward reform of the state (in contrast to the original Deobandi focus on reforming the individual and society) did not emerge fully-formed when the Jamaat was founded in the early 1940s. It was shaped profoundly by the creation of Pakistan.

1947-69: State formation and Islamic identity. The opening years of Pakistan's history were a formative period for the country's two major Islamist movements, the JUI and the JI, each of which wrestled with their role in the first modern "Islamic state." Once the religious parties came to terms, politically speaking, with the creation of the state of Pakistan, they set out to influence its early development as an Islamic institution. The Jamaat, though small numerically, was particularly influential in this regard in the first two decades.

Early attempts by the JI and the JUI to give the new state a substantive Islamist character were, on the whole, unsuccessful. Many of their failed efforts, however, set the pattern for future Islamist strategies of political agitation. For example the Tehrik-e-Khatam-e-Nabuwat (Movement for the Finality of the Prophethood), which pressed for the government to declare the Ahmadiyya sect as non-Muslim, was harshly suppressed by the government in 1953; but by 1974, after significant public pressure by Islamist groups, its main objectives had been accommodated in the form of a constitutional amendment.

The Jamaat's early experiences of confrontation with the martial state would also anticipate its future interaction with the military and bureaucratic elite. When Governor-General Iskander Mirza declared martial law in October 1958 and appointed General Ayub Khan as Chief Martial Law Administrator, he did so in part to thwart the designs of the Jamaat and its growing involvement in the political process.[9] And when Ayub Khan took control from Mirza later that same month and inaugurated his own martial law government, the result was the banning of political parties. Although Maududi chose to follow a pragmatic path that avoided direct confrontation with the military regime—perhaps because he was aware of the fate of the Muslim Brotherhood in Egypt—the Jamaat remained one of the fiercest opponents of Ayub's martial rule.

The basic political orientation of the Jamaat during the Ayub era was pro-democracy, anti-militarist, and above all, anti-secularist. It resented Ayub's modernist experimentation, which ran almost directly counter to its vision of the ideal Islamic state. The party's antipathy toward secularism in the Ayub era was part and parcel of its antipathy toward the West. Maududi saw the secularizing trends in the Arab and Persian world, and feared that, with America's help, the Ayub regime was charting a similar course. In language which very much foreshadowed the Jamaat's rhetoric four decades later, he claimed in 1960 that America "[does] not want Muslim nations to remain Muslim"; that the Americans "most unscrupulously…support dictatorships against democracy"; and that their policies are "possessed by the devil called Jewry." In spite of his strident opposition to the atheism of the communist bloc, he concluded that the Western countries "loom upon Islam as a greater menace than communism."[10]

On the whole, Ayub's tenure was an era of vociferous rhetoric by the religious parties, but minimal Islamist influence. The 1965 war with India brought the Jamaat and Ayub onto the same page for a short while, but it was only a temporary convergence of interests. The Islamists' influence would begin to change in the decade that followed.

1970–77: Islamists and electoral politics. The late 1960s and early 1970s saw the rise of leftist politics in Pakistan, led by Zulfikar Ali Bhutto and his Pakistan People's Party (PPP). The religious parties, forced to confront the emergence of a new mass politics, split on the question of socialism: the more politically-minded (Madani faction) Deobandis insisted that socialist thought was basically in resonance with the populism and anti-imperialism of the pre-Partition Jamiat Ulema movements, while the less politically-active (Thanwi faction) Deobandis and, especially, the Jamaat-e-Islami claimed that socialism amounted to *kufr* (infidelity). The Madani Deobandis were ultimately more adept at aligning their politics with the leftism of the time, and did so in a way that established patterns of JUI politics which continue to the present day.

Few expected that it would be Mufti Mahmud who would take up the mantle of leftist Deobandi politics in Pakistan. Born in 1919, he studied at a Deobandi seminary in Muradabad in the United Provinces, where he became involved in the JUH before returning north to teach at a *madrasa* in Mianwali, a Pashtun-dominated district adjacent to Dera Ismail Khan. During the 1940s, the Mufti formed close ties with the pro-Congress Maulana Husain Ahmad Madani, and began building a political base in his home district. By the late 1960s, the Mufti had inherited the socialist-leaning Madani wing of the JUI, and had developed an active Pashtun constituency in the southern NWFP and the tribal agencies.[11]

When it came time for the 1970 elections, Mufti Mahmud's JUI did not fare particularly well, with one notable exception: the Mufti himself managed an upset victory over Zulfikar Ali Bhutto, chairman of the PPP, in the hotly contested national assembly seat from Dera Ismail Khan. The Mufti's political stature and influence among the JUI *ulema*, particularly in the Frontier, paid off once Bhutto came to power as President in late 1971. Seeking to form a government, Bhutto, Mufti Mahmud, and Wali Khan of the National Awami Party (NAP) signed a Tripartite Agreement in 1972 that set up a joint JUI-NAP government in NWFP. On May 1, 1972, Mufti Mahmud was sworn in as chief minister.

The JUI-NAP government was not to last for more than ten months. It was, however, the first instance of a religious party coming to power in Pakistan, and it served as a high water mark for Deobandi influence in the political arena. Mufti Mahmud's agenda as chief minister would set the tone for the next 30 years of JUI politics. He began a vigorous Islamization program, banned alcohol, introduced an Islamic reform of the inheritance law, and mandated the observance of Ramadan. He further (though unsuccessfully) set out to grant interest-free loans, establish an *ulema* advisory board, make reading of the Qur'an and study of Arabic compulsory for university admission, require women to be veiled in public, insist that the *shalwar-kamiz* tunic be mandatory for government servants, ban dowry, and prohibit gambling.[12]

The Mufti's tenure was brief and unsuccessful, but once his government fell he seemed not dissuaded in the least. His politics in the final years of Bhutto's democratic era involved proposing increasingly sweeping and stringent Islamic-oriented legislation, including anti-blasphemy amendments to the constitution. In 1974, he took the lead with Maulana Yusuf Binori of the famous Madani-influenced Binori *madrasa* in Karachi, to once again raise—this time successfully—legislation that would declare Ahmadis to be non-Muslims.

By the time Zia ul-Haq took power in 1977, the JUI of Mufti Mahmud had grown into a serious and vociferous political voice. Its association with the socialist PPP and its simultaneous use of Islamist rhetoric and promotion of a *sharia* agenda led many to dismiss it as hypocritical, expedient, and cynically pragmatic. But the early reticence by Madani Deobandis to create an Islamic society "from above" had been washed away by the opportunities that Partition presented to redefine their politics and make themselves newly relevant to state and society.

1977–88: Zia ul-Haq and Islamization. General Zia ul-Haq seized power in a coup in July 1977, and quickly declared martial law. His tenure marked a period of tremendous expansion of Islamist influence in Pakistani politics, the contours of which are now well known. The Jamaat's domestic policy during this era was consumed with the question of whether to give precedence to Zia's program of Islamization, or to hold to the party's democratic principles and insist on civilian governance. After much internal disagreement, Maududi's successor Mian Tufail decided that the opportunity to do away with Bhutto and institutionalize the *sharia* program of the Jamaat was too appealing to pass up: the party became a partner with Zia, and contributed several cabinet members to his government.[13]

The Jamaat's governance experience during the early years of the Zia regime was, on the whole, disappointing. Aside from Khurshid Ahmad, who promoted new policies for *zakat* and banking, the ministers were unable to stir the federal bureaucracy into implementing their *sharia* agenda. Their influence was more pronounced, however, in the Council of Islamic Ideology, where Jamaat nominees helped formulate a new package of Islamic penal reforms; and, most of all, in the military, where they were given unprecedented access to the senior officer ranks.

The years of the Afghan jihad under Zia are often characterized as the heyday of the Jamaat, and in a sense they did represent the apex of the party's influence in official circles. But the narrative linking military rule and Islamic politics is not as clean cut as some observers would make it. Just as there was sporadic and symbiotic manipulation between the military and the religious parties during the Ayub era—punctuated by periods of outright hostility— so the relationship between Zia and the Jamaat played out in complex and ambivalent ways. Even in the heady, early days of the jihad, some elements within the party were less than enthusiastic about the martial government. By 1982, the relationship had begun to sour. Zia was feeling more confident in his support from the U.S. and from the *ulema*, and at the same time grew more concerned about the potential for the Jamaat to mobilize its student base against him.[14] After the 1985 non-party elections, in which Jamaat-affiliated candidates performed poorly, the split was complete. The results demonstrated to Zia that the Jamaat had lost its influence, and he turned to other parties for popular support.

The JUI had a much more limited interaction than the Jamaat with Zia's government; by the early 1980s, the JUI, like the JI, was disillusioned with Zia's reforms and began agitating for a return to civilian rule. But the Deobandis were ultimately shaped in profound ways during the Zia era through their participation in the Afghan jihad, and by the patronage they received from the state. The campaign against Soviet forces in Afghanistan resulted in the establishment of hundreds of *madrasas* throughout the Frontier. Not only did the *madrasas* proliferate, but their quality deteriorated markedly throughout the 1980s, and jihadi ideology became more important than mastery of traditional scholarly subjects.

The jihad also began to change, in basic ways, the role of the *ulema* in Pashtun society. Traditionally, the village mullah did not have a separate political role outside the scope of his religious duties.[15] The *ulema* were able to operate in a political role only if they managed to leverage their religious credibility in the pursuit of power politics. The real legacy of the Afghan jihad is to be found not only in the proliferation of the *madrasa*-as-franchise culture of the 1980s, but in the alim-as-entrepreneur culture which followed it. Lower-level *ulema* benefited only indirectly from state patronage during the jihad; following the end of the war and the withdrawal of foreign involvement, these poorly trained clerics—a product of the theologically shallow *madrasas* that had proliferated throughout the province—found themselves unemployable, or at least discouraged by the bleak prospects available outside of the jihadi line of work. These *ulema*, Vali Nasr argues, "began to stake out their own claim to power and wealth—satiating appetites for power, status and wealth that Islamization had whetted but left unsatiated."[16]

The second-order effects of the emergence of this new class were also, in retrospect, of great import. Both the prestige and the external financing which came with the jihadi vocation began to upend the traditional social order, particularly in the tribal areas. Tribal elders, including those maliks who served as paid liaisons between the tribes and the state's political agent, found their standing undermined by new groups of entrepreneurial youth. This trend dovetailed with the explosion of remittance income from the Gulf states in the 1970s, which further reshaped in dramatic ways the political economy of the tribal areas. The systems of indirect rule which the state had relied upon for over a century began to deteriorate in the face of new regional and economic realities.

The Afghan jihad, and the political-economic shifts which it occasioned, opened the door to new forms of Islamism in the Frontier. It brought to the forefront a new clerical class, largely Deobandi in orientation, which was both more diffuse and more ideologically entrepreneurial than its antecedents. It was these "petty *ulema*"—many of whom had only loose connections to the scholarly Deobandi establishment—who in part carried on the most destructive aspects of the jihad into the post-Zia era: the proliferation of small arms and the development of the so-called "Kalashnikov culture," the entrenchment of sectarian movements and their ideologies-of-difference, and perhaps most dangerously the creation of a vast cadre of both ideological and opportunistic veteran jihadis beholden in only the most tenuous fashion to the state system.

The jihad also fundamentally reshaped the demographic profile of the Frontier. The influx of refugees from Afghanistan, beginning in the early 1980s, eventually reached staggering figures; many estimates put the number above 3 million.[17] Peshawar, once dominated by speakers of Hindko (a Punjabi dialect) was soon filled with Pashto-speaking Afghans who quickly overwhelmed the education and social service capacity of the provincial government. This "Afghanization" of the Pakistani Frontier was complemented by the constant stream of foreigners who passed through Peshawar during the 1980s, seeking to stoke the jihad and serve as facilitators for pan-Islamist cadres in their own countries. The broad international participation in jihadi activity in the Frontier in the 1980s foreshadowed the post-9/11 environment, in which the Frontier would once again become a proving ground for young "religious" militants from far-flung corners of the Muslim world.

1988-93: Political realignments. The first two civilian governments which came to power in Islamabad after more than a decade of martial rule faced a host of problems in asserting dominance over an entrenched military-bureaucratic complex. This was a period of relatively minimal political involvement for the Deobandi clerics, and one of indecision for the Jamaat, which was torn between its anti-martial idealism and the pressures of political expediency.

Benazir Bhutto's PPP garnered a plurality of votes in the elections held after Zia's death in 1988, and managed to form a government in the face of a rival electoral alliance orchestrated by the ISI—the Islami Jamhuri Ittihad (IJI)—which included the Jamaat and pro-military mainstream parties. Even in defeat, the IJI parties continued to be a thorn in Bhutto's side: her government, which lasted less than two years, was hobbled by the awkward power-sharing arrangement with President Ghulam Ishaq Khan and Chief of Army Staff Aslam Beg, as well as local competition from Punjab Chief Minister Nawaz Sharif.

The Jamaat, though it had played a major role in the IJI's election campaign, was never entirely comfortable with its place in the pro-military alliance. In 1987 Qazi Hussain Ahmad took over leadership of the Jamaat. Under his leadership the Jamaat retained its ideological focus on Islamization, but broadened its political agenda to include populist agitation and more rhetoric on socio-economic issues. The Jamaat played a vocal but relatively insignificant role in the five years following the return to democratic rule. Its politics were almost consistently contrarian.

New Islamist movements (1993–99). The final six years of democratic governance in the late 1990s saw second terms for Benazir Bhutto (1993–96) and Nawaz Sharif (1996–99). Both the Deobandis and the Jamaat played foundational roles during this era in facilitating the emergence of new Islamist movements.

The most visible of these new movements was the Taliban, led by Mullah Muhammad Omar and seeded from the extensive network of Deobandi *madrasas* which had sprung up in the Pakistani frontier after the Afghan jihad. As noted above, the jihad not only resulted in a proliferation of *madrasas*, but spawned a new, entrepreneurial class of clerics whose ties to the Deobandi establishment were informal at best. Many of the talibs (students) who eventually joined the Taliban movement had studied at Sami ul-Haq's Dar ul-Haqqania *madrasa* outside of Peshawar, and many others at Madani Deobandi *madrasas* in Karachi. At the time, JUI leaders went out of their way to highlight their connections with, and influence over, the burgeoning Taliban movement.

In reality, their influence on the new movement was overstated; they had been overtaken by the entrepreneurial character of Deobandi politics in the Frontier. It was the poorly educated, ideologically hardened, disenfranchised *ulema* who formed the core of the movement. Responding to this trend, the traditional leaders had gravitated toward the role of broker, trading on access, influence, and rhetoric to mediate between institutions (governments, *madrasas*, political parties) and the organic movements themselves.

Although the Jamaat was not at the forefront of the Taliban's advance into Afghanistan, it did play a role indirectly in the emergence of another Islamist movement during this period. The Tehrik-e-Nifaz-e-Shariat-e-Muhammadi (TNSM), or Movement for the System of the *Sharia* of Muhammad, was established in 1989 in district Dir, part of the Malakand administrative division in the Frontier province's northern, mountainous region. The region which became known as Malakand division was originally constituted by princely states; these independent states acceded to Pakistan in 1969. But by the mid-1970s, there was agitation in district Dir over the rights of local merchants to timber royalties, and a local movement formed which demanded a return to the more favorable legal status quo which was operative before 1969.[18]

In response to the demands from Malakand division, Zulfikar Ali Bhutto imposed a new system of tribal law in the area. This system, in turn, was challenged in the Peshawar High Court by lawyers from Malakand, and was eventually overturned. The legal wrangling created an opening into which

Maulana Sufi Muhammad, the first amir of the TNSM, rallied members of the movement to demand *sharia* as the proper successor to tribal law. The movement was also, not surprisingly, able to rally local smugglers and timber merchants to the cause.[19] The Maulana and his followers were not highly educated ideologues in the traditional mold of the Jamaat, but they did have linkages to the JI, and their focused insistence on the implementation of *sharia* was resonant with the party's political approach.

Eventually the state relented to the TNSM's demands, and in May 1994 promulgated a *sharia* ordinance for Malakand which was to remain in effect for four months. The TNSM conducted further protests after the ordinance expired, and the conflict turned violent. Eventually, an agreement was reached between the TNSM and the government in which the state adopted a hands-off approach to the areas around Malakand. The new *sharia* system resulted in few *de facto* changes to the structure of governance, and the state avoided intrusive taxation policies which might inflame local "religious" sentiment. The policy was effective in muting the impact of the TNSM for seven years. Only following the U.S. invasion of Afghanistan after 9/11 was the movement again able to mobilize around a cause.

1999-2001: A return to military rule. Pervez Musharraf's coup in October 1999 brought a return of military rule. The government's support for the Pashtun Taliban was extensive, and state intelligence services also provided a protective cover over al-Qaeda members operating in Pakistan, including the North-West Frontier.[20] The state's support for the Taliban, much of which was covert, was facilitated in part by the Pakistani religious parties, most notably the Deobandi JUI.

The Jamaat, by contrast, had considerably less political investment in the Taliban movement and realized that, for all of the state's support for Taliban and Kashmiri Islamist proxies, Musharraf would be unlikely to make even half-hearted attempts at expanding the reach of Islamist legal or political influence. The party thus conducted protests following the coup.

Evaluating patterns of Islamic politics. There are several recurring themes which emerge from the ways in which Islamic politics, and religious parties in particular, have developed in Pakistan. These patterns form an important contextual backdrop to understanding the rise of the MMA in 2002, and the subsequent fragmentation of Islamism in the Frontier.

One pattern is mutual manipulation. Much has been made of the Pakistani army's use of Islamists. This nexus, commonly known as the "mullah-military alliance," is seen to be at the heart of the state's duplicity with respect to Islamic militancy—i.e., its history of selectively empowering and undercutting Islamist actors in the pursuit of political ends. Though this story contains a great deal of truth, the "mullah-military" nexus is a more complicated story than commonly portrayed. It is a relationship anchored in mutual manipulation, and one which has produced at least as much antagonism as cooperation. The military often used the Islamists for domestic or foreign policy ends, but it is also evident that the Islamists were not infrequently at odds with Pakistan's martial regimes. The religious parties bitterly opposed Ayub Khan, and even the partnership with Zia ul-Haq's government was relatively short-lived. By the mid-1980s the relationship had soured and groups like the Jamaat were again deeply disillusioned.

Second, as might be expected from any political movement, the Islamists have a long history of leveraging external events in order to advance their political standing. This was true for both the Deobandis and for the Jamaat, though they tended to focus on different regions and issues. The Jamaat has historically focused more exclusively on Kashmir, while the Deobandi groups have focused on both Kashmir and Afghanistan.

Third, Islamist movements have been forced to respond to the shifting character of their own constituencies. This is especially true for Islamist parties that depend on electoral support from particular demographic blocs. The early Deobandis, for example, had a long history of interaction with *madrasas* in Afghanistan and the tribal areas, but the movement did not begin as one dominated by ethnic Pashtuns. The Afghan jihad accelerated the process of "Pashtunization" among the Deobandi parties in Pakistan, a process which has resulted in the emergence of JUI factions which often put greater emphasis on ethnic and regional issues than on the broader implementation of Islamic revivalism throughout Pakistan.

Fourth, prior to 2002, Pakistan's Islamists had put forward a very poor showing in electoral politics. They were fringe players at best in parliament, garnering no more than 12% of national assembly seats.[21] Even their parliamentary high water marks were not especially substantive: the 1970 Mufti Mahmud government in NWFP collapsed after less than a year; the Jamaat received cabinet positions in the early years of the Zia ul-Haq regime, but made little headway outside of some Islamic banking reforms; and Maulana

Fazlur Rehman was given the chairmanship of the Foreign Affairs committee during the second Benazir Bhutto government, but implemented no significant policy changes. In spite of this limited success in the electoral arena, Islamist parties have exerted an influence disproportionate to their electoral strength. This has come about in large part because of their effectiveness at mobilizing their political bases, and their skill at using Islamic identity and Islamist goals as "wedge issues."

Fifth, there have been divergent Islamisms. Though Islamism in Pakistan is frequently portrayed as something of a monolith, the reality is more multi-faceted. Even the two major Islamic political blocs, the Jamaat and Jamiat Ulema-e-Islam (Fazl) (JUI-F), have distinctly different visions of an Islamic state and society, and have often been at odds with one another. The JI's outlook is deeply ideological, modernist, and pan-Islamic. Its urban middle-class constituents are primarily concerned with restructuring the legal and political order. The JUI-F, by contrast, is a relatively pragmatic party with a rural, clerical constituency whose objectives are to protect the *madrasa* system from state interference and promote a conservative interpretation of Pashtun social values which they defend as Islamic. It should come as no surprise that these two movements have often found themselves on different sides of the political space in Pakistan and, prior to 2002, did not join together in any meaningful way to advance a common agenda.

THE MMA'S ISLAMIST GOVERNANCE

The Frontier today faces a new and troubling array of insurgent threats. Religious parties like the JUI-F and the Jamaat appear to have been eclipsed by new movements, and no longer set the tone for Islamist discourse. Why then is a narrative of the MMA's tenure still relevant?

It matters for two reasons. First, even though the religious parties are no longer in a governing role, and no longer command the influence they did several years ago, the relationship between mainstream "democratic Islamists" and the new insurgent movements is a critical dynamic in understanding Islamism in the Frontier. Second, the MMA constitutes a worthwhile case study of Islamist governance in practice. There are few instances in South Asia in which Islamists have moved from an oppositional and agitational role to one of actual governance. The dynamics of this shift can reveal important clues about the ways in which Islamist leaders change—rhetorically, politically, and organizationally—when they are forced to interact with domestic and foreign interlocutors. In this respect, the experience of the MMA may be able to shed light on both the promises and the limits of the political process in bounding the more problematic aspects of Islamism, particularly in a Pakistani context.

The Rise of the Muttahida Majlis-e-Amal. The rise of the Islamist alliance in 2002 cannot be understood apart from the American invasion of Afghanistan in late 2001, which immediately became the cause célèbre of the religious parties, and gave them an electoral issue with strong regional, ethnic, and religious appeal. Not surprisingly, Pashtun religious politicians were well positioned to make use of "Islamic rage" in the wake of American operations against the Pashtun Taliban in Afghanistan.[22] In retrospect it appears natural that these politicians and their respective religious parties would coalesce into an alliance opposing the American war in Afghanistan; but in fact the parties had a long history of dysfunctional interaction, and had never before formed a broad-based Islamist alliance. In the year preceding 9/11 there were signs that such an alliance was increasingly possible, but it seems to have taken prodding from former ISI chief Hamid Gul to coalesce the Islamists into a Pak-Afghan Defense Council, which in 2002 became the basis for the Muttahida Majlis-e-Amal (MMA) electoral alliance.[23] The six-party alliance brought together the Pashtun-dominated JUI-F and JUI-S; the Jamaat-e-Islami; the Jamiat Ulema-e-Pakistan, a Barelvi party led by Maulana Shah Ahmed Noorani; the Jamiat Ahl-e-Hadith, a Saudi-influenced Wahhabi party led by Sajid Mir; and the Islami Tehrik-e-Pakistan, a Shia party led by Allama Sajid Naqvi.

The domestic situation was also unusually favorable to the Islamists. President Musharraf had instituted governor's rule in the NWFP after his 1999 coup, and the 2002 polls were to be the first general elections since 1997. Two parties which had traditionally been dominant in the Frontier—the PPP and the Pashtun nationalist Awami National Party (ANP)—were both weak, fragmented, and demoralized. The MMA alliance also benefited from support by the state, which recognized that the Islamists could serve as a useful proxy by which the Musharraf government could decapitate its chief political rivals in the Frontier.

The role of the Pakistani security services in the 2002 NWFP elections has been much disputed. Some commentators have suggested in retrospect that the Islamists' victory was entirely engineered by the ISI; the reality is that the manipulation was significant but subtle. Rather than engaging in large-scale electoral manipulation, the services chose to stifle the mainstream parties while allowing religious leaders a free hand in capitalizing on the wave of anti-American sentiment in the Frontier.[24]

The Islamization program: ambitions and realities. At the heart of the MMA's campaign in 2002—and at the heart of observers' fears about its implications—was its program of Islamization. The MMA constituent parties had played on broad-based sympathies for the Taliban in their 2002 electoral success, and had an ongoing and multivalent relationship with both the Taliban and Kashmiri militant groups. There was almost universal fear following the 2002 polls that the MMA would institute a process of "Taliban-ization" in the frontier areas. Although the MMA made efforts to assuage the fears of the diplomatic and minority religious communities in particular, its chaotic first year in power did little to quell concerns that it represented a subversive and destabilizing force in Pakistani politics.

Expectations were high when the MMA formed its government in the Frontier in October 2002. The nascent government was under public pressure to show quick results on its promises relating to Islamization, anti-corruption, and social welfare. The Islamists' first year, however, was nothing short of chaotic, as interest groups within the Islamist fold began taking action on their own in "support" of the alliance's mandate. The result was what one official described as "rampant ad-hocism," characterized by a flurry of mostly symbolic actions: opening with the *azaan* (call to prayer) in the provincial assembly; banning alcohol, even to non-Muslim foreigners; prohibiting the playing of music in public buses; announcing a crackdown on "pubs and gambling dens" (despite the fact that there were no pubs in the province), etc.[25] Alongside these official moves came a rise in vigilante-style campaigns against "obscenity" in Peshawar and other major cities. Many of these vigilante Islamists had low-level connections to the youth organizations of the MMA parties, and while the Islamist government occasionally criticized these incidents, it did not vigorously investigate them.

Thrust into the spotlight, the MMA leadership also quickly became frustrated by its inability to expeditiously roll out its Islamist agenda. The provincial bureaucracy pushed back against a number of MMA initiatives. By and large, the bureaucracy considered the MMA's early attempts at Islamization to be unrealistic, outside the jurisdiction of the provincial government, or in contravention to existing law. Even the MMA's signature Shariat bill, which was passed unanimously by the provincial assembly and signed into law by the governor, did virtually nothing to advance a substantive Islamization agenda in the province.

The chaos of the MMA's first foray into governance, combined with rampant vigilantism and the specter of new Islamization programs, had by mid-2003 led to severe strains on the Islamist alliance. Concerned about the law and order situation in the Frontier, the ruling party in Islamabad had threatened to impose governor's rule, and was pressuring the MMA to accept the Legal Framework Order which Musharraf needed to legitimate an extension of his dual role as president and chief of army staff. Moreover, the international donor community, led by the World Bank, was on the verge of pulling back support from the Frontier.[26]

Just when it looked as though the MMA's tenure would be as fleeting as that of its ideological predecessor Mufti Mahmud (who ruled for a mere 10 months) the religious alliance stepped back from the brink, and slowly began moving toward a more pragmatic tack. By late 2003, it was evident that the vigilante campaigns had lost momentum, the flurry of Islamist directives had slowed, and the provincial government seemed increasingly interested in orienting its efforts toward development work and securing international donor participation to support its concrete objectives in the sectors of health, education, and infrastructure. This shift was not sudden. But it is clear in retrospect that late 2003 represented a critical inflection point at which the MMA leadership began pivoting toward an Islamism that was decidedly more populist, and more practical.

The Hisbah bill as political drama. The most visible of the MMA's Islamist legal reform initiatives came well after the passage of the mostly-symbolic Shariat Act in 2003. The Hisbah ("accountability") bill was first proposed shortly after the MMA's election victory, but was not presented in the provincial assembly for almost two and a half years. The Hisbah bill played on the themes of Islamic justice and accountability. Some of its less contentious provisions would have discouraged beggary and the employment of under-age children; prohibited injustices perpetrated against women in the determination of inheritance; and banned honor killings. Most of these initiatives, however, were redundant with existing legislation at the provincial or federal levels.

At the heart of the bill was a more controversial initiative: the bill would establish the office of *mohtasib*, a "qualified religious scholar" serving as an ombudsman, to which citizens could refer complaints about the presence of "un-Islamic" behavior to the province.[27] The *mohtasib* would be given subpoena-like powers to requisition documents and compel witnesses and, under some early readings of the language, would have a separate police force at his disposal.

Much to the MMA's disappointment, the international community was deeply skeptical about the legislation. Aware of this growing concern, the Islamist leadership sought to reassure those who saw Hisbah as an attempt to re-create Mullah Omar's Afghanistan. In the end, the Hisbah bill was passed twice by the provincial assembly, and each time was referred to the Supreme Court, where it was struck down on grounds of being "vague, overbroad, unreasonable, based on excessive delegation of jurisdiction, denying the right of access to justice to the citizens and attempting to set up a parallel judicial system."[28] Even though the bill never became law, it came to symbolize the imbalance of power between the NWFP and the ruling party in Islamabad; the difficulty of crafting Islamic legislation that does not run afoul of existing law; and the ways in which the Islamists' own legal inexperience doomed a piece of legislation which, somewhat more narrowly tailored, might have stood a reasonable chance of implementation.

Even so, many observers suspected that both the Islamists and the ruling government in Islamabad were happy to keep the Hisbah issue alive throughout the MMA's tenure. President Musharraf used the legislation to summon the specter of Talibanization in the Frontier, presenting his government of "enlightened moderation" as the only bulwark standing against an imminent Islamist onslaught. And the repeated rejection of the Hisbah bill both created and nourished the Islamists' own rhetoric, allowing the MMA to keep alive the claim that true *sharia* law was just around the corner.

Security, militancy, and inaction. One of the most salient criticisms of the religious government in Peshawar had less to do with its Islamization program than with the ways in which the MMA's stated agenda and constituent politics affected its ability to carry out its law enforcement obligations. Opponents claimed that the MMA leadership was often reluctant to take action against insurgent groups, or even against clerics who were causing trouble for local authorities. By and large, this was true.

Provincial bureaucrats who worked closely with the MMA government described how the Islamists' own rhetoric made them hesitant to act against even those clerics who were not formally part of their religious alliance. This dynamic was most problematic during the first year of the MMA's rule, in which religious party cadres engaged in vigilantism; and in the last two years of the MMA's tenure, in which new insurgent groups began challenging the writ of the state. For most of the MMA's tenure, this remained a relatively minor problem; the law and order situation in the Frontier between mid-2003 and mid-2005 was quite good relative to other provinces, and disturbances by religious groups were relatively few. But with the rise of the TNSM and neo-Taliban-linked bombings in 2006 and 2007, the MMA's hesitance in confronting religious insurgents began to have tangible and adverse implications.

By the spring and early summer of 2007, the religious parties were coming under severe criticism for their indecisive response to the TNSM's militancy in Swat, and to a wave of bombings which had penetrated into the settled areas of the province.[29] Politicians from the religious parties unconvincingly blamed the federal government and its security services, rather than the Taliban groups, for fomenting instability in the Frontier to destabilize the MMA government. The situation in NWFP further deteriorated in the summer of 2007 following retaliations by militant groups after the siege of the Lal Masjid (Red Mosque) in Islamabad. The MMA government put off any kind of action against the TNSM until the final weeks of its rule, when the JUI-F chief minister quietly agreed to an expanded security presence in the Swat valley. Even then, the JUI-F did so reluctantly and in the face of internal opposition by the Jamaat, and later denied that it had ever acceded to allowing military action in Swat.

It is an overstatement to suggest, as some observers have, that the rise in militancy in 2006 and 2007 in NWFP was a result of the MMA provincial government. At the same time, however, the MMA clearly played an indirect role in facilitating the spread of the insurgency by virtue of its inaction.

Gender, religious minorities, and sectarianism. It was widely expected that the rise of the MMA would lead to the imposition of strict gender norms, even by the conservative standards of the Frontier. But despite the MMA's views on the role of women in public life, its impact on the gender policies of the province, and on the norms of the society at large, were relatively modest. Aside from a few abortive attempts to mandate the wearing of head coverings for female students, the alliance's education and health policies basically supported the status quo on gender issues. Any greater ambitions to institutionalize enforcement of gender norms died with the repeated failure of the Hisbah bill.

Opposition to the MMA by women's advocacy groups moderated somewhat over the course of the provincial government's tenure, as the religious parties became more realistic about their policy options, and the advocacy groups calibrated their expectations accordingly. The alliance's gender policies nonetheless continued to attract criticism on two fronts. First, there were charges that the religious parties were interfering with gender-oriented programs: MMA leaders, for example, campaigned against the Aurat Foundation, which they saw as advancing a Western notion of female empowerment.[30] And second, perhaps the most substantive complaint about the MMA's approach to gender issues was its consistent opposition to legal reforms on issues which affected women. The religious parties opposed any change to the notorious Hudood ordinances in 2004, and strongly resisted the Women's Protection Bill in 2006.

The religious leadership was frequently torn between its own commitment to conservative gender norms and political realities. Faced with local constituent opposition to women's participation in politics (especially in rural areas), but also with the desire to fill the seats which were reserved for women, the Islamist leadership split the difference: MMA women were given tickets to run for seats at the district and provincial levels, while at the same time the religious parties occasionally went along with local agreements at the union council and *tehsil* (administrative unit within the NWFP local government system) levels to exclude women from voting. After a writ petition was filed following the 2001 Local Body Elections, citing written evidence of prohibitions against women voting, these sorts of arrangements tended to be oral rather than written.

As for religious minorities and sectarianism, the NWFP has historically experienced less conflict between Muslim and non-Muslim communities than neighboring Punjab. Minority groups in NWFP were uniformly concerned about the MMA's victory in 2002, but the MMA's impact on minority communities, as on so many other issues, proved to be mixed. Contrary to early expectations, the religious parties did not seek to further marginalize minority groups. In fact, the MMA leadership, concerned about its collective reputation and by the suggestion that it might act irresponsibly toward religious minorities, tried to overcome this negative optic by reaching out to minority leaders, particularly those from the Christian, Hindu, and Sikh communities. The outreach was largely symbolic, but nonetheless important in setting the overall tone of the MMA's interaction with minority communities.

These outreach efforts did not make the MMA immune from criticism. Some Christian leaders objected to the MMA's oft-repeated assertion that they would "protect" the minorities living under their rule, arguing that the language of dhimmitude was patronizing and cast the minorities as somehow less than full Pakistani citizens. Other leaders noted that the MMA leadership often dismissed the minority groups' claims of discrimination, and did little to provide economic opportunities to the poorest communities.

There is, remarkably, little to note about the MMA's track record on sectarian issues. On the whole, the alliance adopted moderate rhetoric toward the Shia minority, and did its best to stay out of the middle of intra-Sunni disputes between Deobandis and Barelvis which arose in nearby Khyber agency.

On balance, the minority communities in the Frontier were relieved that the MMA's tenure was not as problematic as they had feared, and expressed satisfaction with official efforts at outreach on the part of the Islamist leadership. But they also were frustrated over the actions of lower-level Islamist cadres which the leadership did not or could not control, and over the trend toward more conservative values under the MMA, which increased the social pressures on communities which did not conform to the Deobandi Sunni norm.

Constraints on Islamization. The portrait that emerges here is that of the MMA as a right-of-center but essentially status quo political force. And indeed, as early as 2004 it had become obvious that the Islamist parties would not be a radical Talibanizing influence in the Frontier. While their policies and rhetoric continued to trouble many observers, the religious parties were clearly unwilling or unable to press for dramatic Islamist reforms.

One reason for this was internal alliance politics. From its earliest days, the MMA was an alliance fraught with internal divisions. These fractures played out differently at the local, provincial, and national levels. At the local level the differences between the two dominant parties were not related to strategic objectives so much as jostling for influence: both parties' operatives in a given district sought to take advantage of the political environment for their own ends. At the provincial level, disputes predictably centered around the distribution of patronage, including cabinet positions, in which the JI and especially the smaller parties in the alliance felt excluded. Somewhat less expected was that the pace of the MMA's Islamization agenda would also prove to be a point of provincial-level contention within the alliance. And at the national level, the JUI-F and JI shared relatively little in the way of overall objectives, and saw the relationship between the MMA and the state through starkly different lenses.

Another salient factor which limited the MMA's ability to implement its Islamist agenda was the lack of enthusiasm for real reform within sectors of the MMA's own constituency. An overwhelming majority of Pakistanis, when surveyed, express support for "implementing strict *sharia* law" in Pakistan.[31] Actual implementation of strict regulations ostensibly deriving from the *sharia* is decidedly less popular. Even the relatively modest changes implemented by the MMA in NWFP provoked grumbling—and not just among "liberal-minded" Pashtuns.

But the mild character of the MMA's Islamism is often explained with reference to a single factor: its manipulation and cooption by state elites. Of all of the variables which constrained the MMA's Islamist agenda, this was arguably the most critical. Beginning with the MMA's victory in the NWFP, in which the state itself had a hand, there were profound pressures on the provincial Islamist government to comply with the interests of the martial regime in Islamabad.

Politically, the central government held several key levers of control over the MMA. It appointed the province's chief secretary and inspector general of police, and its approval was required for large development projects. Islamabad was also able to hold out the prospect of governor's rule if the religious alliance did not comply with the central government's wishes. The Musharraf government also exerted pressure on the religious alliance at the federal level, and retained enormous financial leverage over the MMA government.

That said, it is too simplistic to dismiss the MMA as nothing more than "puppets" of the central government. Like all political blocs in Pakistan, the MMA found itself constrained by the interests of the ruling elite, and by a system which limited the ability of any one party to significantly change the balance of power between civil and military institutions. But Musharraf's ruling party also had its own political imperatives: virtually devoid of allies in the NWFP, it needed the MMA government's support, and benefited both from the perception of a democratic order, and from fears in the West of a resurgent Islamism in the Frontier.

NEW ISLAMISTS AND THE RETURN OF PASHTUN NATIONALISM

During the final years of the MMA's governance (prior to its defeat in the 2008 polls), its standing was affected not only by its relationship with the Musharraf government, but by the advent of two important trends: first, the rise of new Islamist actors in the Frontier, commonly known as the neo-Taliban; and second, the return of Pashtun nationalism. It is still too early to present a robust history of the Frontier's new insurgent movements and their relation to the Islamist political establishment. What began in mid-2006 as a spillover of militancy from the troubled Waziristan tribal agencies into NWFP's southern settled districts became within about a year's time a movement which threatened the political stability of the entire Frontier.[32]

This new movement, known as the neo-Taliban, is distinct from both the Afghan Taliban and from mainstream Pakistani Islamists such as the MMA, though it has critical linkages with both groups. "Neo-Taliban" is itself a term of convenience, and refers not to a coherent operational entity but rather to a loose collection of self-defined Taliban groups which share a number of common features. To the extent that one can generalize about this new form of insurgent Islamism, it can be seen as having several distinguishing characteristics.

First, the movement is politically rejectionist. Unlike the mainstream Islamist parties, neo-Taliban groups tend to dismiss the legitimacy of the Pakistani state, either for ideological reasons or on account of the state's ostensible failure to live up to its Islamic political commitments. On this point, however, the movement is far from monolithic. Groups with close ties to al-Qaeda, such as some Taliban organizations in Waziristan and Bajaur, are more likely to have a transnational Islamist outlook and clear ideological reasons for rejecting the Pakistani state's legitimacy. Other more locally-oriented movements, such as those which emerged in Swat district and Khyber agency, tend toward a language of vigilante Islamism, in which they accept the state's role in theory but legitimize violence on the basis of its ostensible failings. Needless to say, the latter groups are more amenable to political compromise or cooption, provided that they do not fall under the sway of the former.

Second, the neo-Taliban tend to be more *takfiri* in their ideology than the mainstream Islamists: that is, they are more willing to sanction jihad against other Muslims who reject their sectarian or ideological position. (They claim, of course, that these other groups are in fact not truly Muslim.) Mainstream Islamist parties do frequently operate along sectarian lines, but are inclined to outsource sectarian violence to affiliate groups in order to retain their democratic credentials. This ideological split is also deeply political: the religious parties in the Frontier recognize that *takfiri* ideology can easily boomerang back upon the more mainstream Islamists. They have, as a result, tried to pre-empt this ideological and political move against them by repeatedly rejecting the legitimacy of suicide bombing within Pakistan (though their position with respect to other locales is less clear cut).

3. Third, the movement is often linked to criminal networks and the illegal economy. This was, and remains, true for the Afghan Taliban, which is intimately linked to the opium trade. In the Pakistani context, it is becoming increasingly clear, even to the public at large, that the groups which call themselves Taliban are often no more than armed gangs which use religious symbolism to gain a foothold in local communities. Whereas mainstream religious parties such as the JUI-F historically maintained side interests in local transport networks, the neo-Taliban groups have explicitly sought to dominate local services and industries, particularly in the FATA and PATA regions.

4. Fourth, these groups are highly entrepreneurial. The creation of Tehrik-i-Taliban Pakistan (TTP) in late 2007 merely formalized what had become a franchise-oriented model of insurgency. And while the Tehrik eventually took on a coordinating role among the various Taliban groups, it succeeded as a brand more than as an organization. TTP's branding strategy sought to portray the movement as cohesive, and affiliate it with a simple platform of religious and political values. This aggregation function served the TTP leadership in Waziristan by amplifying its voice and reach, but also served the local affiliates by providing them with access to resources, and by discouraging local communities from pushing back against outsiders who claimed to be part of the umbrella organization.

5. Fifth, the Taliban groups have proven adept at coopting the state at the local level. Their expansion has often followed a predictable pattern: well-armed groups of young men enter an area with Kalashnikovs and white pickup trucks, calling themselves Taliban; they win the favor of the community by taking on local criminal elements and prohibiting certain un-Islamic behaviors; they establish *qazi* courts for the quick adjudication of disputes; and, having garnered some measure of local support, they set about solidifying their control by marginalizing or killing local notables and government officials, enacting even stricter Islamist measures, and establishing environments conducive to their criminal networks. By playing off of local discontentment with the judicial system, policing, and other state services, the insurgents are able to gain a foothold which they use to reinforce their local position.

6. Finally, this new movement is increasingly in tension with traditional Pashtun norms. While at a macro level, the neo-Taliban movement is a

Pashtun-dominated insurgency, the insurgents also threaten established norms by killing tribal elders, carrying out suicide bombings, and attacking jirgas. Other aspects of Pashtun culture are amplified perversely by the militants: the destruction of girls' schools, barber shops, and music stores sit uncomfortably with most Pashtuns living in the conservative southern districts of the NWFP.

Vigilante Islamism and the mainstream-militant divide. The nature of the relationship between this new insurgent Islamism and the mainstream religious parties is not well understood. Commentators in the West have tended to assume that the similar rhetoric of the two groups reflects a commonality of objectives, tactics, and even organizational structures. It is true that the political discourse of neo-Taliban insurgents is often close to that of parties like the JUI-F and the Jamaat, and that just as the religious parties during the MMA era retained linkages to militant Islamist groups, so they continue to interact informally with the neo-Taliban movement. Nonetheless, these commonalities belie very important differences.

The fault-lines began surfacing in 2006, but only came to the forefront in 2007 when neo-Taliban groups began challenging the state in places like Swat, Bannu, and even Islamabad. It was, in fact, the Lal Masjid (Red Mosque) crisis in the summer of 2007 that exposed deepening rifts between the religious parties and the vigilante Islamism of the new Taliban groups.[33] The Jamaat, for example, was outspoken in its support for the Lal Masjid leadership, but—to its shock—found itself disowned by the *madrasa* students who were challenging the government's writ in Islamabad. The JUI-F tried to serve in a mediating role between the state and the militants, but ended up receiving criticism from its own ranks for not supporting the *madrasa* against "interference" by the state. More significantly, a rift formed within the JUI-F regarding the proper response to vigilante Islamism of the kind carried out by Abdul Rashid Ghazi and his students at the Lal Masjid. Even before the government's operation against the *madrasa* students in July, dissenters within the JUI-F (many of whom were from the Baluchistan wing of the party) had argued that they needed to come out strongly in favor of the Taliban groups. Fazlur Rehman and most senior JUI-F party members from the NWFP demurred. After the operation, the conflict burst into the open, and the JUI-F leadership wrestled for several months with internal dissenters who insisted that the party was obligated to support the *madrasas* and the Islamization agenda of the neo-Taliban.

Links between the JUI-F and Taliban groups have been well documented, particularly in the southern part of the province where Deobandi politics is strong.[34] But the rise of the insurgency in 2006 and the aftermath of the Lal Masjid crisis in 2007 further complicated the nature of JUI-F interaction with the neo-Taliban and other vigilante Islamist groups. By early 2008, this relationship had become extremely complex.

The new Islamist "moderates." The rise of new Islamist groups over the last several years has served to marginalize the religious parties, but also change their role. Many religious party leaders are now "moderates" within their own Islamist context in the Frontier. Although they share some of the same objectives as the new insurgent groups, their inclination to reject vigilantism and to support the democratic political order marks them as being more similar to mainstream political actors than to militant groups.

Although the religious parties have been weakened, they continue to occupy an important political space between Islamist militancy and relatively liberal democratic norms. Even secular observers interviewed in Peshawar in 2007 and 2008 expressed concern that the religious political establishment— leaders like Fazlur Rehman and Qazi Hussain—might lose their ability to draw young activists into the formal political space rather than see them join militant organizations. The religious parties relish the opportunity to play the part of intermediaries between the militants and the state, and will likely continue to do so. Their views on the legitimacy of violence and vigilantism are also apt to prove important means by which they distinguish themselves from more militant Islamist efforts.

Ultimately, the marginalization of the religious parties is likely to induce two contradictory responses. On the one hand, the parties will be pressured to distance themselves from the rising tide of Islamist militancy, both as a means of retaining their democratic legitimacy, and protecting themselves from new (and violent) forms of political competition. On the other hand, the religious parties will face pressure to compensate for their diminished stature by moving further to the right in an attempt to motivate their political base, and insulate themselves from *takfiri* accusations.

The 2008 Frontier elections. Despite an array of problems, the February 2008 general elections were widely acknowledged as being the fairest since 1970.[35] Postponed following the assassination of Benazir Bhutto in December

2007, the polls were held amidst growing anger at the Musharraf government, and growing fears about extremist influence. The voters delivered a resounding defeat to Musharraf's PML-Q, and at the national level a clear narrative emerged tying the election results to a rejection of Musharraf's rule and an embrace of the mainstream democratic politics of the PPP and Nawaz Sharif's PML-N.

In the Frontier the results appeared to tell a different, but related, story. The MMA was defeated soundly by its rivals, garnering only 10% of provincial assembly seats (down from about 50% in 2002). The Pashtun nationalist ANP delivered the strongest showing, with 32% of seats, followed by independent candidates with 23%, and the PPP with 18%. The PPP-S, PML-N, and PML-Q each polled about 5%. On the strength of their combined showing, the ANP and PPP formed a governing coalition which was supported by the PPP-S and the independents.

The electoral success of the ANP and PPP brought about a flood of news reports hailing the rise of secularism and the rejection of religious politics and "Talibanization" in the Frontier. While this narrative captured one important dynamic of the poll results, it did not tell the entire story. The religious parties' defeat was due to a number of factors. Public anger over American action in Afghanistan was no longer a driving force as it had been in the 2002 elections, and anti-Western sentiment was no longer the province only of the religious parties. Moreover, the MMA's standing had been weakened by rifts within the alliance over the extent of its cooperation with Musharraf's military government, and following the imposition of the Emergency in late 2007, the JI had decided to boycott the elections. The mainstream and nationalist parties were also given much wider latitude to contest the elections than in 2002, and there was significantly less government interference in the election process.

At a more granular level, the February 2008 results can be seen as the product of four separate trends in voter behavior, each of which played a role in shaping the outcome. The first trend was one of specific opposition to the MMA. Part of the anti-MMA vote was tied to concerns about the alliance's ineffectual response to creeping militancy in the NWFP. Many voters felt that the religious government was too sympathetic to the new Taliban movements to be able to respond decisively to security threats in the province. At the same time, MMA also lost credibility with its conservative religious constituency, which was upset that the alliance had not done enough to implement a program of *sharia* in the province.

The second trend was of general opposition to the MMA. Anti-incumbency has traditionally been a powerful determinant of voter behavior in the Frontier: The ruling party nearly always loses in the NWFP. In part this is attributable to voter frustrations about corruption and ineffective governance, but in part it reflects a systemic problem. The provincial government's role in the Pakistani federation is such that it does not have sufficient autonomy or resources to allow incumbents to deliver on most of their promises. In this case, the MMA's undoing was in large part its perceived failure to deliver on education, health, and clean government—the same things that brought down many of its predecessors. That the Islamists raised expectations by promising to be righteous and incorruptible simply reinforced voter disenchantment.

The third trend was one of specific support for the ANP and PPP. Both of these parties ran on platforms promising to deal with the rising militancy in the Frontier, and the ANP in particular was able to draw on its heritage of non-violence and its reputation for relatively competent governance. The ANP had rebuilt its party operations after years of internal strife, and was able to mobilize strong patronage networks.

The fourth and final trend was one of general support for the ANP and PPP. As Andrew Wilder has argued, voting behavior in Pakistan is often driven less by policy considerations than by public perceptions about which candidate or party is most likely to win.[36] Since voters rely on their representatives for political favors and patronage, it is in their interest to vote for winners rather than simply for those who share their political outlook. In the run-up to the 2008 elections there were widespread expectations, voiced in the media, that the ANP and PPP would return strong showings in the NWFP polls, and the PPP would be the leading party at the national level. This incentivized local voters to cast their lots with these parties.

While none of these factors can easily be quantified, one can make a case that the general trends described above carry with them a more robust explanatory power than any specific anti-MMA or pro-ANP/PPP sentiments. The historical salience of anti-incumbency voting patterns, combined with the strong trend toward voter bandwagoning with expected winners, should give pause to those who would see the 2008 elections as a resounding defeat for religious politics, or an embrace of secular Pashtun nationalism.

Taking the long view, the MMA's defeat in 2008 is best seen as a return toward the mean, in which political fragmentation in the NWFP is the norm rather than the exception. What does this mean for the religious parties in the

Frontier? Both the JUI-F and the JI used their five-year tenure to gain valuable experience into the workings of government and are likely to remain significant, but not dominant, players in the NWFP political scene. An MMA-like alliance may prove useful to these parties in the future as a means of amplifying their collective influence in the national political debate. But that being the case, the trend toward a party system in Pakistan with two dominant mainstream parties and a number of smaller religious and ethno-nationalist parties makes it likely that the JI and the JUI-F will each prefer to adopt a more flexible and independent electoral strategy so that they can remain free to bargain their way into a mainstream alliance after voting has taken place.

CONCLUSION: TOWARD POLITICAL MAINSTREAMING

U.S. policymakers dealing with the Frontier are routinely torn between short-term objectives, which are primarily oriented around preventing attacks on U.S. forces in Afghanistan, and America's long-term interest in seeing a stable Frontier that denies Islamist insurgent groups the physical and socio-political space to carry out operations against Pakistan and its allies. This mismatch unavoidably entails certain trade-offs between counterterrorism and counter-insurgency objectives. Ground incursions by U.S. troops into the FATA, for example, may disrupt key terrorist networks, but also undermine long-term efforts to stabilize the Frontier.

In general, though, these tradeoffs are far from absolute. Despite wide-spread militancy and growing concerns about Pakistan's strategic ambivalence regarding the neo-Taliban insurgency there is no reason the U.S. cannot pursue a two-track approach that addresses the short-term terrorist threat and at the same time lays the groundwork, even incrementally, for more comprehensive counterinsurgency efforts. This approach is critical because solutions to the problems posed by illiberal or insurgent Islamism ultimately require political mainstreaming. This, in turn, calls for legitimate and capable state institutions—both civilian and military—which can set the political boundaries for Islamist participation and respond effectively to new and unexpected forms of "religious" insurgency.[37]

To begin with, a successful counterinsurgency track will be able to leverage political and social fragmentation in the Frontier. The Pakistani government has a long history of taking advantage of cleavages within and among tribal structures.[38] In the wake of the "Anbar Awakening" in Iraq, American policymakers have discussed whether similar strategies might be successful in Pakistan. Carrying out a tribe-oriented Anbar model in and around the FATA would pose real challenges on account of the internally fragmented, egalitarian, and increasingly entrepreneurial nature of the Pashtun tribal system. Although tribal lashkars may prove to be useful in pushing back neo-Taliban advances in some areas, and should be supported by the state when they do so, these *ad hoc* alliances are likely to disintegrate quickly or even turn against the government.[39] Any effort to take advantage of fragmentation in the Frontier must integrate political strategy with tactical approaches from the outset, and should be oriented around a concerted program to incentivize tribal communities and relatively moderate Islamist groups to integrate into the political mainstream.

Ultimately, the cleavages that matter most are those that divide politically accommodationist groups which accept the authority of the state from politically rejectionist groups which contest it. This is true within tribal communities as well as within ideologically-driven Islamist movements. And here again, the U.S. can play a significant but indirect role by supporting policies that help to delegitimize and isolate rejectionist groups, and encourage local populations and relatively moderate Islamist leaders (such as those who supported the "old" Taliban but are threatened by the neo-Taliban movement) to throw in their lot with the state rather than the insurgents.

This requires the use of "soft power" initiatives, particularly in the area of FATA development. But it also requires that such initiatives be more thoroughly integrated with security efforts and robust governance reforms. Integrated approaches—even if they are, at first, implemented only in small demonstration areas—are likely to be the only effective means of translating development assistance into support for state authority.

These policies will obviously take time. But their potential impact is not confined to the long-run. They can also have immediate relevance as a means of assisting the government of Pakistan in solidifying its near-term military gains in the Frontier. The United States as a practical matter has no choice but to work with Pakistan in addressing the rise of the neo-Taliban, and laying the groundwork for a more comprehensive and holistic strategy.

ENDNOTES

1 Pakistan's Frontier is managed under a complex and sometimes baffling patchwork of governance systems, many of which were inherited and adapted from British times. For a detailed background on these systems, see Daniel Markey, *Securing*

Pakistan's Tribal Belt (New York: Council on Foreign Relations, Aug. 2008), pp. 3-10; Joshua T. White, "The Shape of Frontier Rule: Governance and Transition, from the Raj to the Modern Pakistani Frontier," *Asian Security*, Autumn 2008; and Naveed Ahmad Shinwari, *Understanding FATA: Attitudes Towards Governance, Religion and Society in Pakistan's Federally Administered Tribal Areas* (Peshawar: Community Appraisal & Motivation Programme, 2008). For the purpose of this monograph, the term "Frontier" is taken to include both the North-West Frontier Province (NWFP), which is governed by an elected provincial government in Peshawar; and the Federally Administered Tribal Areas (FATA), which operates under the oversight of the federal government through the office of the governor in Peshawar.

2   Examining these and other challenges, a bipartisan group concluded in September 2008 that "we find U.S. interests in Pakistan are more threatened now than at any time since the Taliban was driven from Afghanistan in 2001." Pakistan Policy Working Group, *The Next Chapter: The United States and Pakistan*, Sept. 2008, p. 1.

3   See especially Sana Haroon, *Frontier of Faith: Islam in the Indo-Afghan Borderland* (New York: Columbia University Press, 2007); Ayesha Jalal, *Partisans of Allah: Jihad in South Asia* (Cambridge, MA: Harvard University Press, 2008).

4   See Olaf Caroe, *The Pathans: 550 B.C.–A.D. 1957* (Karachi: Oxford University Press, 2006 [1958]), 364–69.

5   For a detailed look at the lasting influence of the Akhund's pirimuridi line, see Haroon, *Frontier of Faith*, p. 43ff.

6   Barbara D. Metcalf, *Islamic Revival in British India: Deoband, 1860–1900* (Princeton, NJ: Princeton University Press, 1982), p. 86.

7   See, e.g., Zia ul-Hasan Faruqi, *The Deoband School and the Demand for Pakistan* (London: Asia Publishing House, 1963), pp. 110–11.

8   This phrase is borrowed from Gilles Kepel. See Gilles Kepel, *Jihad: The Trail of Political Islam* (Cambridge, MA: Belknap Press of Harvard University Press, Anthony F. Roberts trans., 2002).

9   Seyyed Vali Reza Nasr, *The Vanguard of the Islamic Revolution: The Jama'at-i Islami of Pakistan* (Berkeley: University of California Press, 1994), chapter 7.

10   Interview with Chiragh-e-Rah, Karachi, Dec. 1960, in Sayyid Abul 'Ala Maududi, *Selected Speeches & Writings of Maulana Maududi* (Karachi: International Islamic Publishers, S. Zakir Aijaz trans., 1982), pp. 62-64.

11   For a lively history of Deobandism in the Frontier, and the role of Mufti Mahmud, see Sana Haroon, "The Rise of Deobandi Islam in the North-West Frontier Province and its Implications in Colonial India and Pakistan 1914–1996," *Journal of the Royal Asiatic Society* (2008).

12   This is a partial list. See Sayyid A.S. Pirzada, *The Politics of the Jamiat-i-Ulema-i-Islam Pakistan 1971–1977* (Karachi, New York: Oxford University Press, 2000), p. 67.

13   Mumtaz Ahmad, "Islamic Fundamentalism in South Asia: The Jamaat-i-Islami and the Tablighi Jamaat of South Asia," in *Fundamentalisms Observed* (Chicago: University of Chicago Press, Martin E. Marty & R. Scott Appleby eds., 1991), p. 480.

14   Ibid., p. 483.

15 Erland Jansson, *India, Pakistan or Pakhtunistan: The Nationalist Movements in the North-West Frontier Province, 1937–47* (Uppsala, Stockholm: University of Uppsala, 1981), p. 59.

16 Seyyed Vali Reza Nasr, "The Rise of Sunni Militancy in Pakistan: The Changing Role of Islamism and the Ulama in Society and Politics," *Modern Asian Studies* (Feb. 2000), p. 150.

17 For a discussion of refugee numbers, see Daniel A. Kronenfeld, "Afghan Refugees in Pakistan: Not All Refugees, Not Always in Pakistan, Not Necessarily Afghan?," *Journal of Refugee Studies* (Mar. 2008).

18 See Pakistan Institute for Peace Studies, "TNSM: A Taliban Like Movement," Aug. 15, 2007; Muhammad Amir Rana, "Backgrounder: Shariah Movement in Malakand," Pakistan Institute for Peace Studies, Apr. 29, 2008.

19 The TNSM reportedly had deep linkages with the grey economy in Malakand. See Pakistan Institute for Peace Studies, "TNSM: A Taliban Like Movement."

20 See Ahmed Rashid, *Descent into Chaos* (New York: Penguin, 2008), p. 48ff.

21 Frédéric Grare makes this point forcefully in his paper, "Pakistan: The Myth of an Islamist Peril," Carnegie Endowment for International Peace, Feb. 2006.

22 Khaled Ahmed, "Three Angry Pushtuns," *Friday Times*, Aug. 16, 2002.

23 See, e.g., M. Ilyas Khan, "Inside the MMA," *Herald*, Nov. 2002. Hamid Gul was later described as a "strategic advisor" to the MMA, and in 2006 was involved in an unsuccessful attempt to create a more hardline Islamist alliance which would include organizations of a more militant character than the JI and JUI-F. Arnaud de Borchgrave, "Gulled by Gul," *Washington Times*, Dec. 2, 2004; Hasan Mansoor, "New Religious Alliance in the Offing?," *Daily Times* (Pakistan), Mar. 11, 2006.

24 See "Government Helped MMA Leaders Contest Elections," *Daily Times* (Pakistan), Nov. 8, 2002.

25 Author interview with a provincial government official, July 2007, Peshawar. See, e.g., *Express* (Urdu), Nov. 28, 2002. These restrictions generally did not apply to the cantonment areas, which operated under the control of the military. As a practical matter, however, private enterprises in the cantonment, such as hotels, chose to abide by the MMA's restrictions.

26 In June 2003 a World Bank official was quoted as saying: "We feared the Talibanisation of Pakistan soon after the MMA came to power. Its recent moves have further strengthened our apprehensions. We are now fully convinced that the Alliance is hell-bent on enforcing the Taliban system on Pakistan." Mohammad Shehzad, "MMA Causes US$200 Million Loss," *Friday Times*, June 20, 2003.

27 The MMA justified the introduction of the *mohtasib* on the grounds that the other three provinces in the federation had already established such a position. While this was technically the case, the role of the *mohtasib* as envisioned in the Hisbah legislation far outstripped the largely symbolic *mohtasib* positions that had previously been established in other parts of Pakistan. In other respects, the bill's establishment of the *mohtasib* office was simply redundant (Musharraf's Local Government Ordinance of 2001, for example, allowed for *mohtasibs* at the district level).

28 "Opinion of the Supreme Court in Reference No. 2 of 2005 (PLD 2005 SC 873) [Hisba Bill case]," Supreme Court of Pakistan. See also Mohammad Kamran, "SC Declares Key Hasba Sections Unconstitutional," *Daily Times*, Aug. 5, 2005.

29 See, e.g., Ismail Khan, "Govt's Writ Weakening in NWFP, Tribal Areas," *Dawn*, Mar. 29, 2007; Raza Khan, "An Intensified Talibanisation," *Weekly Cutting Edge*, May 9, 2007; David Montero, "Pakistan Losing Territory to Radicals," *Christian Science Monitor*, May 29, 2007.

30 See "NGO Accuses MMA Govt of Coercion, Ends Collaboration," *Dawn*, June 12, 2003; "Lack of Islamic Teachings Blamed for Crime Against Women," *Daily Times*, Jan. 24, 2004.

31 See the August 2007 and January 2008 surveys by Terror Free Tomorrow, which reported that about three-quarters of respondents said that "strict *sharia*" was "very important" or "somewhat important." A survey conducted in September 2007 by World Public Opinion also reported that 75% of respondents thought that *sharia* should play "a larger role" or "about the same role as it plays today" in Pakistani law. C. Christine Fair et al., "Pakistani Public Opinion on Democracy, Islamist Militancy, and Relations with the U.S." (WorldPublicOpinion.org and United States Institute of Peace, Jan. 7, 2008).

32 See, e.g., Behroz Khan, "Settled NWFP Areas Also Under Threat of Talibanisation," *The News*, Sept. 30, 2006; Nicholas Schmidle, "Next-Gen Taliban," *New York Times Magazine*, Jan. 6, 2008.

33 For a more detailed analysis of the religious parties' response to the Lal Masjid crisis, see Joshua T. White, "Vigilante Islamism in Pakistan: Religious Party Responses to the Lal Masjid Crisis," *Current Trends in Islamist Ideology* (Autumn 2008).

34 See, e.g., Imtiaz Gul, "The Fog of War in Waziristan," *Friday Times*, Mar. 17, 2006

35 For a balanced summary of the election process, see Democracy International, *U.S. Election Observation Mission to Pakistan General Elections 2008: Final Report*, May 2008; and reports by the Free And Fair Election Network (FAFEN), available at http://www.fafen.org.

36 See Andrew R. Wilder, *The Pakistani Voter, Electoral Politics and Voting Behaviour in the Punjab* (Oxford: Oxford University Press, 1999).

37 A recent study examining how terrorist groups end concluded that politicization and policing were the two most important reasons, accounting for 43% and 40% of the cases respectively. "Victory" and military force accounted for a combined total of only 17%. Seth G. Jones & Martin C. Libicki, *How Terrorist Groups End: Lessons for Countering al Qa'ida* (Santa Monica, CA: RAND, 2008), p. 18ff.

38 Recently, the state has also worked to separate local groups from foreign influences. See, e.g., Sadia Sulaiman, "Empowering 'Soft' Taliban Over 'Hard' Taliban: Pakistan's Counter-Terrorism Strategy," *Jamestown Terrorism Monitor*, July 25, 2008; Rahimullah Yusufzai, "A Who's Who of the Insurgency in Pakistan's North-West Frontier Province: Part One—North and South Waziristan," *Jamestown Terrorism Monitor*, Sept. 22, 2008.

39 The historical dimension of conflict in the FATA is often overlooked in journalistic accounts. As Joshua Foust has noted, "Missing from the excited calls for another 'Awakening' movement is an understanding of Pakistan's history before it was Pakistan. Tribal unrest, even Islamist-fueled tribal unrest, is a regular and cyclical occurrence." Joshua Foust, "Did We Just Invade Pakistan?," *Columbia Journalism Review*, Sept. 26, 2008.

5 | Afghanistan's Flawed Elections: Implications for the Insurgency[1]

by C. Christine Fair

On August 20, 2009, Afghanistan's public went to the polls amidst serious security concerns. U.S. officials, among others, prematurely applauded both the poll's success and the transparency of the process.[2] Within days of that early optimism, it was clear that the electoral process had suffered serious defects. There were irregularities and problems with the voter registration update. The campaign period was marred by violence, driving candidates underground along with their staff and rendering recruitment of electoral and campaign staff incredibly difficult—especially women. Within weeks of the election, the Afghan Electoral Complaints Commission (ECC) reported that it received 3,051 complaints, including complaints related to problems that arose during the campaign period.[3] Of these complaints, 893 were deemed serious.[4] Preliminary results released in September suggested that incumbent Hamid Karzai received 54% of valid tallied votes. Had he sustained this majority, Karzai would have avoided a run-off, and remained Afghanistan's president for the next five years.

Yet many suspected that his lead was ill-gained. Having investigated allegations of fraud, the ECC had already cancelled the ballots of some polling stations in Ghazni, Paktika, and Kandahar provinces, all in the Pashtun belt in the south, by mid-September. Given the ECC's limited resources, it took nearly two months for the commission to investigate the numerous cases before it. However, a run-off did not seem likely. Based on the results of 91% of the polling stations, more than 400,000 votes for Karzai would have to have been annulled to precipitate a second round of voting.[5] However, in the end nearly one in four ballots cast in August were disqualified.

On October 21, 2009, the Independent Electoral Commission (IEC) announced that after investigating allegations of fraud, President Karzai had received 49.67% of the total valid votes. This was a decrease of 4.95 percentage points from the preliminary results. His main rival, Dr. Abdullah Abdullah, received 30.59% of the total valid votes, an increase of 2.8 percentage points from the preliminary results. Since no candidate received more than 50% of the votes, a run-off was necessitated, and the IEC set November 7 as the run-off date.[6] Amid overt and covert discussions of a "coalition" arrangement, and after decrying international interference, Karzai acquiesced to a run-off. Ultimately Dr. Abdullah withdrew, arguing that the run-off would be no fairer than the August 20 vote because the government did not make personnel changes to the IEC demanded by Abdullah, among other reasons.

This chapter discusses the contexts and outcome of Afghanistan's flawed August 2009 presidential elections. Critically, it lays out several implications for the United States and NATO as they struggle to stabilize Afghanistan and defeat, through various means, an insurgency that has only intensified since 2005.

The chapter is organized as follows. First, it describes how security shaped the contours of the election's credibility. Second, it exposits the impacts that the security situation had on the electoral process from beginning to end. Third, it examines security on election day itself, and the importance of this factor for the credibility of the exercise. Fourth, it lays out a number of implications for the Afghan insurgency, and the counterinsurgency effort. It concludes with a discussion of U.S. policy options in light of the twin challenges of deepening insurgency and rapidly deteriorating confidence in Kabul.

SECURITY: SHAPING THE CREDIBILITY OF THE 2009 ELECTIONS

Since 2005 in particular, the Taliban and allied anti-government elements have continued to consolidate their positions in Afghanistan's south, southeast, and east, and have steadily made inroads into areas of the north such as Kunduz, Baghlan, Badghis, and Faryab. In May 2009, according to the United Nations, there were more than 1,000 security incidents in Afghanistan—the first time this happened in a single month since 2001. Mid-way through 2009, there was a 43% increase in monthly security incidents relative to 2008.[7] In 2008, out of more than 350 districts in Afghanistan (not all district boundaries are agreed upon), the government did not control ten and access was restricted in another 165.[8] This situation has likely worsened since 2008.[9]

Given the escalating insecurity in the months leading up to the presidential elections, which were initially scheduled to take place in May 2009, concerns raged inside and outside Afghanistan about the capacity of the Afghan government and its international allies to conduct a maximally credible electoral exercise, especially in the most insecure parts of the country.[10] Ultimately, after protracted discussion and deliberations, the Independent Election Commission (IEC) announced in late January that the elections would be postponed until August, citing security among the key factors justifying the delay.[11] With the impending arrival of an additional 21,000 U.S. troops, the delay allowed those troops to arrive in theatre before the rescheduled election.[12]

The delay was ultimately sanctioned by the Afghan government, and ameliorated the concerns of those domestic and international analysts who feared that the security environment would inhibit the Pashtun vote, thereby raising a different set of credibility issues. Needless to say, the Pashtun belt is also where Karzai expected his strongest support. Despite initial beliefs that the postponement made sense, international stakeholders soon realized that they were now in an awkward position. With Karzai's legal tenure lapsing in May, coincident with the onset of the insurgents' fighting season, the international community needed to support "government continuity." Many Afghans—possibly including President Karzai himself—interpreted this as tacit support for the incumbent. Efforts to dispel the notion failed to impress Afghans, or were seen as U.S. efforts to find a new alternative. The net impact is that many Afghans suspected that the election was an exercise reflecting Washington's interests—as Taliban propaganda claimed.

SECURITY: IMPACTS ON THE ELECTION PROCESS

Unexpectedly, the voter registration update process was relatively pacific. Security incidents were few but serious: registration centers could not open in eight districts (five in Helmand, two in Ghazni, and one in Wardak).[13] Reportedly, registration was nominal or limited in large swathes of the south and southeast.[14] Registration imposed a definite hardship upon potential voters in insecure areas: an unspecified number of registration centers had to be relocated to nearby districts, and travel to faraway centers would have been difficult for many in the countryside due to Afghanistan's inhospitable terrain and lack of widely available transport.[15] In the end, approximately 4.5 million voters were registered during the registration update, 38 percent of whom were women.[16]

In the run-up to the 2004 and 2005 elections, over-registration was one of the first indications of potential fraud. In 2004, there were some 10.5 million voter cards distributed, which exceeded the estimated number of voters (9.8 million).[17] In some of the most insecure areas such as Nuristan, Khost, Paktia, and Paktika, registration suspiciously exceeded the estimated number of voters by 140%. The 2005 voter registration update added another 1.7 million voter registration cards.[18]

For the 2009 elections, a further 4.4 million registration cards were added, bringing the total number of voter registration cards to an improbable 17 million. The Free and Fair Election Foundation of Afghanistan estimated that about one in five of the new cards went to underage boys, and another one in five was a duplicate. While women's registration was overall low given security and cultural considerations, the number of registered women actually exceeded that of men in some of the most insecure areas. In Paktia, election officials reported that nearly twice as many women than men registered. Given the extreme conservatism that precludes women from leaving the home, it is unlikely that this is a measure of women seizing their legal right to franchise. Men are generally able to obtain voting cards for women simply by supplying a list of women who are alleged family members.[19]

However, insurgent threats continued after the registration update period. Moving into the pre-election period, Taliban leader Mullah Mohammad Omar called for a boycott, arguing that the election would be a U.S.-driven process to produce figureheads acting at Washington's behest. At the local level, anti-government elements issued "night letters" threatening those who voted with beheading.[20] In this phase, election staff were threatened and kidnapped; female workers were particularly vulnerable to intimidation, which made hiring female employees very difficult; and there were isolated attacks on convoys of election materials (i.e. in Wardak), assaults on persons with voter cards at Taliban checkpoints, and the murder of at least two provincial council candidates in May (one in Khost and one in Ghazni). In addition, police were attacked in several incidents near registration centers.[21] Pre-election violence escalated as August neared, with violence and threats of violence against provincial council candidates, members of the IEC, and staff working on various campaign teams.[22] The pre-election security environment forced candidates, campaigners, electoral staff, and voters to limit their mobility and conceal their actions as much as possible. Again, women were disproportionately affected.

SECURITY ON ELECTION DAY

Election security was the primary responsibility of the Afghan National Security Forces (ANSF). The Afghan National Police (ANP) formed the first line of defense of the polling centers, and the Afghan National Army (ANA) formed the second line of defense. ISAF would deploy only *in extremis*.[23] In initial planning stages, "high-risk" polling centers were to receive an allotment of ten police, "medium risk" were to get six, and low risk were to get four. However, with only 86,000 police—up to 30,000 of which were "ghost police"[24]—this structure was impossible. If one assumes an average of 8 police for each of the 7,000 estimated polling stations, some 56,000 police would be required, which is at or in excess of the total end strength of the country's entire police force leaving aside other duties.[25] In some provinces, the shortages of police are striking. In Paktia province, police figures are estimated to be as low as 30 per district, allowing criminals and anti-government forces to act with impunity.[26] Equally problematic, recruitment of female search agents (as well as polling agents) began only a few weeks before the election. Three days before the election, the shortfall for female polling and search agents exceeded 42,000 countrywide.[27]

President Karzai's brother-in-law and head of the Independent Directorate for the Protection of Public Properties and Highways by Tribal Support, Arif Noorzai, developed a 10,000-man national militia program, ostensibly to provide additional security for polling centers largely in the southern Pashtun belt.[28] Opponents of the program were concerned that it was being used in insecure Pashtun areas, and not in non-Pashtun areas that were equally insecure. If the rationale for the program was purely a desire to protect the opportunity to vote for at-risk voters, then one would have expected it to be used elsewhere. More disturbing, the government provided little public information about how this militia would be recruited, used, paid, and demobilized.

Given that the program bore the imprimatur of Karzai's brother-in-law, the possibilities for conflicts of interest were obvious. The lack of transparency and clear connections to Karzai motivated public distrust of the program. (Many Afghans rejected the "solution" of using militias, and preferred that the government recruit and train Afghan police who have an official status and an official chain of command—even if the police are often corrupt and do not serve their constituents.)[29]

Several weeks after the election, there was still virtually no transparency about how many of these militia members showed up on election day, and what they actually did.[30] This fostered suspicion that the militia members—beholden to Karzai and his brother-in-law—engaged in nefarious activities in support of the incumbent.

In addition to the Noorzai initiative, there were several local provincial militia initiatives. For example, the Herat provincial government announced that it planned to recruit 1,000 men who would be armed to help the police on election day.[31] Other provinces also sought to implement some expedited version of the American militia program, the Afghan Public Protection Force (APPF), which Washington has marketed as a "local initiative."[32] The APPF vetted its militia candidates rather thoroughly, with identification and training of members taking several months; some governors wanted to implement militia programs in the immediate run-up to the elections, which would not have permitted the time to properly vet militia members.

While election centers and voters had inadequate security, candidates and workers associated with electoral bodies, human rights organizations, and others were also at risk due to the dearth of security forces. Candidates complained that they had inadequate or no security. Though the Ministry of Interior committed to paying for security details that candidates managed to hire, it wasn't clear how these guards would be armed or how reimbursement would take place. Female candidates and electoral workers were especially vulnerable given the various threats that females face in Afghanistan.

By most accounts, election day itself was relatively peaceful. While no comprehensive publicly available data have been released about the numbers of violent incidents on election day, international sources interviewed by the author suggest that there were between 100 and 250 incidents related to the elections. Given the various kinds of threats in Afghanistan, it is often difficult to determine the motivation of a particular attack and ascribe it to the electoral process rather than a feud or criminal enterprises. But it is clear that the Taliban did not execute a spectacular attack as some had feared. (In both the 2004 and 2005 elections, the Taliban did not execute a spectacular attack either.)

Even though election day was generally peaceful, there were several serious concerns that require additional analysis and understanding. First, the exact locations of polling stations were not revealed until the day before the elections in insecure areas. There were serious differences of opinion between the security forces and the IEC about the disposition of polling centers deemed "unsafe." Such a determination led to either stations remaining unopened (about 10 percent of the 7,000 stations) or being co-located to safer locations. Such arrangements clearly imposed hardship upon voters—either by outright disenfranchising them, or by requiring them to make long journeys to relocated centers. While men may have been in a position to make such a journey, it would have been quite difficult or impossible for women. And, as became apparent in the weeks after the election, such a determination also created opportunities for electoral fraud; worse still, many feared that such moves were used to permit electoral fraud.

Second, the government did little to educate the public about the security arrangements on election day. Many persons interviewed by this author in Afghanistan in the run-up to the election suspected that this may have been deliberate, noting that fewer voters showing up would make any electoral malfeasance easier to execute. Of course, this is unlikely to be true, but perception ultimately matters most: if potential voters anticipated that they would not be secure (irrespective of the actual arrangements) they would be less likely to risk their safety by casting their votes.

Third, because there has been no census since 1974, there is no real way of knowing how many legitimate voters there are in Afghanistan. (The registration update did not remove people who died, for example.) This means that it is impossible to ascertain whether some areas produced turnout that would be impossible given the local population assigned to a particular polling station.

Fourth and related, because of the obvious security constraints on both international and domestic election observers, it was nearly impossible to conduct an independent assessment of actual voter turnout versus ballots returned. Similarly, while domestic observers may have been present in the district capitals and other secure areas, it is doubtful that they could have penetrated remote, insecure areas or those areas which are controlled by so-called commanders, which may include "war lords," Taliban, or other violent non-state actors. In such circumstances, it is doubtful that staff was in a position to enforce fraud-mitigation measures even if they were inclined to do so.

IMPLICATIONS FOR THE INSURGENCY

Going into the elections, there were few outcomes that would have advanced the cause of stabilizing Afghanistan politically or otherwise. Successful counterinsurgency strategy requires that the citizens have some degree of confidence in the government, yet the available data suggests that the contrary is true in Afghanistan. ABC, with BBC, has conducted four polls every year since 2005. The February 2009 poll showed that the percentage of respondents who thought the country was going in the right direction had plummeted from 77% in 2005 to 40%, coincident with the Taliban's resurgence. In the same period, approval for Karzai had declined from 83% to 52%, and support for the Afghan government retrenched from 80% to 49%.[33] While the absolute numbers may not seem terribly alarming,[34] the declining trend line in Afghans' assessment of their president and government is.

As the foregoing data suggest, Hamid Karzai has not been able to gain the confidence of his citizenry. The international community too has grown wary of his ability to steer his country out of danger. He has repeatedly demonstrated a lack of political will to deal with corruption and narcotics trafficking, nor has he found a way of providing better governance. Despite large sums of international assistance, many programs cannot succeed without a committed partner in Kabul. International efforts to build the country's police forces have been hampered by shortages of international human and financial resources. However, they have also been hampered by the political context in which police training takes place. The current program, Focused District Development (FDD), extracts all the police from particular districts and sends them off for training. After completing their training at a police training facility, they return to their district under the guidance of international mentors. However, when the newly-trained police return, the district and provincial governors remain in place, along with other corrupt notables. There is little point in dusting off the police only to re-insert them into the same corrupt networks that helped to foster police corruption in the first place. At a minimum, FDD should be coordinated with replacing corrupt district and provincial governors with more trustworthy stewards of governance. Unfortunately, corrupt governors are rarely retired; rather, they are simply ordered to new districts or provinces, or other desirable government portfolios.

President Karzai has shown repeated insouciance about the country's expanding narcotics problem. Not only are two of his brothers reputed to be heavily involved in the racket, but in 2009 he pardoned five heroin traffickers (in military uniforms) because one of the men was tied to his re-election campaign. As one former U.N. official remarked of this decision, "Karzai is pulling out all the stops in his bid to get reelected."[35]

While the degree to which narcotics proceeds fund insurgents is debated, a recent congressional report claims that the narcotics trade likely provides anywhere between $70 million to $500 million per year.[36] Moreover, the narcotics trade has fostered a network of collusion between insurgents and criminal groups, resulting in a new phenomenon for Afghanistan: the rise of narcotics cartels. Antonio Maria Costa, executive director of the United Nations Office on Drugs and Crime, has noted that "the drug trade in Afghanistan has gone from being a funding source for insurgency to becoming an end in itself."[37] This is in addition to the more quotidian—but equally devastating—effects of corrupting the banking sector, encouraging informal banking transfers, and undergirding the entire economy with illicit funds. It also raises the economic opportunity cost of engaging in any licit agricultural activity, making programs like crop substitution and alternative livelihoods unlikely to succeed.

The electoral process also attested to the degree to which Karzai is motivated by self-interest, and capable of undermining his own base of credibility. While accusations of fraud were widespread against Abdullah Abdullah, Karzai's main rival, the primary onus of demonstrating a clean campaign was on Karzai. As the incumbent, he stood accused of positioning district and provincial governors, and chiefs of police who were positively disposed towards him. He was also accused of using state media to his advantage, among other actions designed to tip the elections in his favor.

The international community—especially the United States—bears some blame. It had long sidelined Karzai and the government in general. Karzai has no control over the international forces operating in his country, and the government has incomplete visibility into the various activities going on in Afghanistan. The sectoral approach to rebuilding Afghanistan has failed in part because each of the activities (security sector reform; governance, rule of law, and human rights; and economic and social development) were deeply vertically integrated. Security sector reform absorbed the vast majority of resources, with the predictable result that the Afghan government still is incapable of providing governance or rule of law, and remains riven by corruption despite the infusion of billions of dollars in aid since 2001. Moreover, it is far from obvious that the instruments of state-building available to the United States and its partners are effective. There are long-standing criticisms of corruption in USAID contracting, leading many to note that for every dollar spent, 90 cents returns to the United States.[38]

At the same time, the international community cannot hold Afghanistan to a different standard than it holds for itself. While it is true that Afghanistan is plagued by numerous law-and-order problems, the international community has shown considerable willingness to undermine Afghanistan's interests by advancing its own, including standing up so-called "grassroots" militias, supporting the postponement of elections, allowing a relative lack of accountability on civilian casualties (although new ISAF commander Gen. Stanley McChrystal may change this), and by pursuing extra-constitutional solutions to Afghanistan's various problems.

The election again put the international community in an awkward position. In the two months following it, it was apparent that Karzai would most likely become the president. Thus some were worried that chastising him would render him less willing to continue cooperating. On the other hand, citizens of donor countries are increasingly asking why their countries are endangering lives and squandering treasure to defend a government that seems indefensible in the wake of elections so blatantly marred by extensive fraud.

MOVING FORWARD: WHAT NEXT?

The international community—even if it were appropriately configured to meet the tasks of rebuilding Afghanistan—is likely unable to "win" in Afghanistan, if "winning" means establishing a competent, reasonably transparent government capable of providing even limited services and eventually being able to pay for itself. The international community cannot succeed without real reformers at the central, provincial and district levels. Gen. McChrystal, while maintaining that the war is "winnable," conceded the importance of governance. His August strategy called for a more intense focus upon diminishing corruption among local officials.[39] While President Obama revised the U.S. goals in Afghanistan in December 2009, much of the strategy still relies upon Karzai's commitment to diminish the corruption which is hindering U.S.-led efforts to build competent Afghan National Security Forces.[40]

Persuading Karzai to address corruption and other governance failings will require political will in Washington, European capitals, and within Kabul and the provincial capitals. Such a focus on governance and corruption will certainly put the international community and Karzai's government on a collision course, as many within his government (including his own near and extended family) are deeply implicated in the country's pervasive drug trade and other forms of criminality and corruption.

Without a capable and reasonably clean and effective government, international efforts to stabilize Afghanistan and reverse the gains of insurgents are not likely to fructify. With current force structures, the international security forces and Afghan forces cannot defeat the Taliban. While they can "clear," they cannot hold, and the Taliban retake the territory as soon as international forces leave. Moreover, a weak, discredited, and ineffective government cannot pursue any sort of accommodation with the Taliban that would either be enduring or on terms favorable to the government. Why would the Taliban acquiesce when it is clear that they have the upper hand?

The larger question that needs to be asked is why the United States is fighting in Afghanistan, expending blood and treasure on what appears to be an impossible task. The justification of "9/11" is inadequate. U.S. operations are not largely focused on al-Qaeda, and more militant threats reside in Pakistan than in Afghanistan. Moreover, the notion that one must stabilize Afghanistan to stabilize Pakistan is misguided. Many of Afghanistan's problems are rooted in Pakistan and Pakistan's strategy for the country. Despite a formal declaration of support for the democratic regime in Kabul, Pakistan fears expanding Indo-Afghan ties, and fears that India will use Afghanistan as a base to squeeze Pakistan. Thus Pakistan continues to seek ways of influencing the events in Afghanistan primarily through covert support of the Taliban. Admittedly, even if Pakistan didn't support the Taliban insurgency, Kabul's own ineptitude would ensure that the Taliban could sustain steady progress in consolidating their base and expanding into new territory where the state is absent or where the population is disaffected.

The long-standing bromide of sending more troops, which has been endorsed by the Obama administration, also appears dubious. While the administration has committed to sending an additional 30,000 U.S. troops to Afghanistan, Afghan support for international forces has declined. Dispatching more troops means more fights with the insurgents, and inevitably more of the civilian deaths that Afghans deeply resent. According to a recent U.N. report on civilian casualties, between January 2007 and December 2007, there were 1,523 civilian casualties. Of these, "anti-government elements" killed 700, compared to "pro-government forces" killing 629. Another 194 cannot be attributed.[41] What is clear is that the pro-government forces are not killing substantially fewer civilians. Worse, more Afghans blame the international forces for the deaths than the Taliban insurgents.[42]

Clearly the United States needs a new strategy, and a plan B. This plan B should not be merely reconfiguring plan A in hopes that it will succeed the second time around. The U.S. government must foster a serious debate about what U.S. interests are in Afghanistan. First, if the objective is al-Qaeda, then it is far from clear how current approaches meet that objective. Indeed, the surge could even undermine U.S. ability to prosecute the war on al-Qaeda. This is because the surge will result in far more than 30,000 additional persons who need to be sustained in Afghanistan through the lines of control in Pakistan. When one considers the increased requirement for civilian contractors and private security among other civilians required to support the announced military and civilian surge, U.S. officials concede that as many as 80,000 additional personnel will be dispatched to Afghanistan.[43]

This suggests that Pakistan—where al-Qaeda is largely ensconced, along with the Afghan and Pakistani Taliban and other al-Qaeda allies—will become more immune to U.S. pressure because of its increased importance in sustaining the war in Afghanistan. How can the United States meaningfully pressure Pakistan to take more aggressive actions against al-Qaeda and its Pakistan-based allies in the tribal areas, North-West Frontier Province, and the Punjab when Pakistan's support has become so much more critical to sustaining the logistical pipeline for the expanded war in Afghanistan?

Unfortunately, Washington announced this troop increase without developing a robust northern supply route. Iran, which hosts alternative ports currently used by some troop contributing countries such as Italy, remains an unpalatable ally for Washington. This position on Iran is puzzling: Iran only aspires to proliferate as Pakistan already has, and Pakistan is also a major sponsor of terrorism. Yet the U.S. has repeatedly undermined its own legal and ideological commitments to nonproliferation and counterterrorism by funneling billions of dollars to Pakistan since 9/11 while being unable to forge even tactical alliances with Iran.

Second, if the objective is state building, and if our state-building tools are inadequate and unsupported by a corrupt and venal government in Kabul, how can sustained expenditure of U.S. human and financial resources be justified? If building Afghan security forces to deal with internal security is the objective, how can this be sustained given that the state cannot pay for even modest portions of the costs of raising and sustaining this military? While Obama's December 2009 plan is a serious retrenchment from McChrystal's August 2009 plan, the United States remains committed to building up the Ministry of Defense and Ministry of Interior despite the above-noted problems.

This essay does not purport to answer these questions; rather, it calls for a redefining of U.S. interests in Afghanistan. Should the goal be to defeat the Taliban? Should it focus upon al-Qaeda? Can the United States secure its interests vis-à-vis al-Qaeda even if the Taliban are not defeated decisively? Once these goals are redefined and communicated to the American public, Washington needs to adopt a strategy and operational plan to achieve these redefined and clarified objectives. Before the United States continues to squander the lives of American armed service personnel and civilians as well as financial resources, these questions need to be forthrightly raised, and debated in a non-partisan way. The American public deserves to understand what the United States seeks to accomplish, and with what resources, in a conflict they increasingly don't understand or support.[44]

ENDNOTES

1 This essay is based on C. Christine Fair, "The Afghan Elections: Who Lost What?," testimony presented before the United States House of Representatives, Subcommittee on the Middle East and South Asia, Oct. 1, 2009.

2 After visiting a limited number of polling stations on election day, Special Envoy Richard Holbrooke declared that the voting he'd seen was "open and honest." See "Afghans Vote Despite Sporadic Violence," *Reuters,* Aug. 20, 2009. President Obama also called the election a success. See "Obama Says Afghanistan Poll a Success," *Reuters,* Aug. 20, 2009.

3 The ECC is reconstituted for every election, and has a limited period of operation before and after the election in question. International election experts and monitors have opined that the ECC should be a permanent body, and have noted that the ECC has been a neglected organization that is ill equipped to deal with the challenges of elections in Afghanistan.

4 Afghan Election Complaints Commission, "Decisions," available at http://www.ecc.org.af/en/index.php?option=com_content&view=article&id=72&Itemid=65 (last visited Oct. 3, 2009).

5 "Fraud Watchdog Annuls Votes in Afghan Election," *Reuters,* Sept. 10, 2009.

6 See United Nations, General Assembly Security Council, "The Situation in Afghanistan and Its Implications for International Peace and Security," Dec. 28, 2009. (These reports are required at regular intervals, and have the same title. They are therefore distinguished by their dates of issue.)

7 See United Nations, General Assembly Security Council, "The Situation in Afghanistan and Its Implications for International Peace and Security: Report of the Secretary-General," June 23, 2009.

8 United Nations, General Assembly Security Council, "The Situation in Afghani-

stan and Its Implications for International Peace and Security: Report of the Secretary-General," Mar. 10, 2009.

9 See, e.g., BBC Online, "Election Security Map," Aug. 19, 2009.

10 Carlotta Gall, "Allies Ponder How to Plan Elections in Afghanistan," *New York Times,* Apr. 11, 2009.

11 "Afghanistan Delays Presidential Election," *CNN.com,* Jan. 29, 2009; John Dempsey & J. Alexander Thier, "Resolving the Crisis Over Constitutional Interpretation in Afghanistan," *USIP PeaceBriefing,* Mar. 2009.

12 Golnar Motevalli, "Extra U.S. Troops in Afghanistan by Mid-July," *Reuters,* May 31, 2009.

13 See International Crisis Group, *Afghanistan's Election Challenges* (Brussels, Kabul: ICG, June 2009), p. 23. The United Nations reported that nine could not open; however, no information about the location of those centers was provided. See United Nations, General Assembly Security Council, "The Situation in Afghanistan and Its Implications for International Peace and Security," June 23, 2009.

14 See Martine van Bijlert, "How to Win an Afghan Election," *Afghanistan Analysis Network,* Aug. 2009.

15 Mobile teams were used to continue registering potential voters, although persons interviewed in Kabul, Herat and elsewhere by the author suggested that persons were not familiar with the mobile registration units.

16 United Nations, General Assembly Security Council, "The Situation in Afghanistan and Its Implications for International Peace and Security," June 23, 2009.

17 As there is no census, the United Nations Assistance Mission to Afghanistan (UNAMA) estimated the potential number of voters by extrapolating information from the 1974 census and other sources. It is possible that UNAMA underestimated the voter population, but it is unlikely that this would explain the large number of registered voters. See van Bijlert, *How to Win an Afghan Election.*

18 Ibid.

19 See Anand Gopal, "Afghan Voter Registration Marred," *Christian Science Monitor,* Dec. 23, 2008; Carlotta Gall, "Fears of Fraud Cast Pall Over Afghan Election," *New York Times,* Aug. 3, 2009.

20 See International Crisis Group, *Afghanistan's Election Challenges,* p. 23.

21 Police have been and remain a frequent target of insurgents due to their vulnerability, exposure, and poor training and equipment. Ibid.

22 The Afghanistan NGO Safety Office, "The ANSO Report," July 1-15, 2009; The Afghanistan NGO Safety Office, "The ANSO Report," July 16-30, 2009.

23 Author meetings with NATO officials in Kabul, Mazar-e-Sharif, Mar. 2009.

24 "Ghost police" refers to police who are on the payroll but who do not actually exist, or do not show up for work. This also intimates fraud whereby someone is collecting the salaries of "ghost police."

25 Author interviews in Kabul, Jalalabad, Herat, Aug. 2009.

26 See International Crisis Group, *Afghanistan's Election Challenges,* p. 23.

27 Jerome Starkey & Kim Sengupta, "Afghan Women to Miss Out on Vote in Landmark Election," *Independent* (U.K.), Aug. 17, 2009.

28 See Rahim Faiez, "Afghanistan Hires 10,000 Tribesmen to Secure Polls," *Associated Press*, Aug. 11, 2009.

29 Author interviews with candidate workers, security officials, human rights and electoral workers in Kabul, Jalalabad, Kunduz and Herat, Aug. 2009.

30 Jessica Weinstein, "Tribal Guards Add Little," *Washington Times*, Aug. 27, 2009.

31 See "Herat Arms Villagers to Secure Voting," Institute for War and Peace Reporting, Aug. 18, 2009.

32 For more information about the APPF, see Institute for the Study of War, "The Afghan National Police," n.d. (accessed Jan. 5, 2010).

33 "Support for U.S. Efforts Plummets: Amid Afghanistan's Ongoing Strife," *ABC News*, Feb. 9, 2009.

34 By the end of his term, U.S. President George Bush had only a 33% approval rating. Nancy Pelosi, Speaker of the House of Representatives, enjoys a meager 18% approval rating. (Unlike the polls of approval of President Bush, a large fraction—47%—either did not know or did not have an opinion of Pelosi.) See CBS, "CBS News Polls: Bailouts, the Economy and the President: March 12-16, 2009," Mar. 17, 2009.

35 Quoted in Farah Stockman, "Karzai's Pardons Nullify Drug Court Gains: Well-Known Traffickers Set Free Ahead of Election," *Boston Globe*, July 3, 2009.

36 *Afghanistan's Narco War: Breaking the Link Between Drug Traffickers and Insurgents*, Report to the Committee on Foreign Relations, United States Senate, Aug. 10, 2009.

37 See Richard A. Oppel, "U.N. Sees Afghan Drug Cartels Emerging," *New York Times*, Sept. 2, 2009.

38 See discussion in C. Christine Fair & Seth G. Jones, *Securing Afghanistan: Getting on Track* (Washington, DC: USIP, 2009).

39 See Stanley A. McChrystal, *Commander's Initial Assessment*, Aug. 30, 2009.

40 See The White House, "Remarks by the President in Address to the Nation on the Way Forward in Afghanistan and Pakistan," Dec. 1, 2009.

41 United Nations Assistance Mission to Afghanistan, Human Rights Unit, *Afghanistan: Annual Report on Protection of Citizens in Armed Conflict, 2008*, Jan. 2009.

42 ABC News/BBC/ARD Poll, "Support for U.S. Efforts Plummets Amid Afghanistan's Ongoing Strife," Feb. 9, 2009.

43 Author interviews with American and Pakistani military and diplomatic officials in Dec. 2009 and Jan. 2010.

44 Only one in four Americans polled in 2009 supported augmenting troops, compared to 45% who want to decrease the military forces there. (Many of the remaining respondents want to keep the level about the same.) More generally, 51% of polled adults believe that the Afghan war is not worth fighting, a figure that keeps rising. Less than half, 47%, believe that the war is worth the costs imposed. And those who strongly oppose the war (41%) outnumber those who strongly support it (31%). See Jennifer Agiesta & Jon Cohen, "Public Opinion in U.S. Turns Against Afghan War," *Washington Post*, Aug. 20, 2009.

6 The Drug-Conflict Nexus in South Asia: Beyond Taliban Profits and Afghanistan

by Vanda Felbab-Brown

Perhaps nowhere in the world does the presence of a large-scale drug economy threaten U.S. primary security interests as much as in Afghanistan. There, the anti-American Taliban strengthens its insurgency campaign by deriving both vast financial profits and great political capital from sponsoring the illicit economy. The strengthened insurgency in turn threatens the vital U.S. objectives of counterterrorism and Afghan stability, as well as the lives of U.S. soldiers and civilians deployed there to promote these objectives. The opium poppy economy also undermines these goals by fueling widespread corruption in Afghanistan's government and law enforcement, especially the police forces.

A failure to prevail against the insurgency will result in the likely collapse of the national government and Taliban domination of Afghanistan's south, possibly coupled with civil war. A failure to stabilize Afghanistan will in turn further destabilize Pakistan, emboldening jihadists and weakening the resolve of Pakistan's military and intelligence services to take on Islamic militancy. Pakistan may once again calculate that it needs to cultivate its jihadi assets to counter India's influence in Afghanistan—perceived or actual.

But the seriousness of the threat, and strategic importance of the stakes, should not lead one to conclude that implementing aggressive counternarcotics suppression measures today will enhance U.S. objectives and global stability. Just the opposite is true: Premature and inappropriate counternarcotics efforts greatly complicate counterterrorism and counterinsurgency objectives, and hence also jeopardize economic reconstruction and state-building efforts. They are also unsustainable in the long term, and indeed counterproductive even for the narrow goal of narcotics suppression.

At least until the new counternarcotics policy that the Obama administration indicated it would undertake in summer 2009—defunding and deemphasizing eradication and focusing on interdiction and rural development—counternarcotics efforts in Afghanistan unfortunately had these undesirable effects.[1] The new policy, if implemented well, promises to redress many of the deficiencies of previous efforts and synergistically enhance counterinsurgency and counterterrorism objectives.

But counternarcotics policies in Afghanistan are also of critical importance for the wider regions of Central and South Asia. The need for a regional approach, especially one that seeks to stabilize Pakistan and prevent the displacement of the narcotics economy into Pakistan, is of urgent and paramount importance. A policy that solely focuses on poppy reduction in Afghanistan without also emphasizing a prevention of poppy reemergence in Pakistan will have serious negative effects on U.S. vital security and geostrategic objectives.

AFGHANISTAN'S POPPY PAINS

Since 2001, Afghanistan has become synonymous with "narco-state," and the spread of crime and illegality. During 2007 and 2008, the Afghan drug economy reached levels unprecedented in the history of the modern drug trade at least since World War II, and so far efforts of the international community and the Afghan government have failed to contain and reduce it. Despite forced eradication efforts, opium production in Afghanistan climbed to a staggering 8,200 metric tons in 2007. Afghanistan supplies 93% of the global illicit market for opiates, and more than 95% of the European market.[2]

The latest United Nations Office on Drugs and Crime (UNODC) survey of Afghanistan's opium poppy economy indicates that cultivation of poppy during the 2008-2009 growing season stood at 123,000 hectares (ha), and opium production at 6,900 metric tons (mt).[3] While both numbers represent a decline from the 2007-2008 growing season of 22% and 10% respectively,[4] both numbers remain very high. Indeed, at 6,900 mt, Afghanistan's total production of opium significantly surpasses the total global estimated demand for illicit opium.[5]

Opium constitutes about one third of the overall economy in Afghanistan.[6] Poppy cultivation thus inevitably underlies much of Afghanistan's economic and political life. The Taliban profits from the drug trade, as do officials in the Afghan police, members of tribal elites, and many ex-warlords-cum-government officials. And of course, poppy feeds much of the rural population and also underpins much of the economic activity in the cities. Corruption is endemic; but so are the micro and macro-economic spillover effects from the poppy economy.

Reinvigorated by a number of factors, including access to safe havens in Pakistan, the Taliban insurgency greatly ratcheted up its attacks in 2007; security has deteriorated to critical levels,[7] not simply in the south and east, but increasingly also in the north. Although the Taliban does not necessarily permanently control territory in these areas, it can generate enough instability to prevent government and international access and paralyze normal everyday life, thus severing the link between the population and the government.

Paradoxically, counternarcotics efforts contributed to the Taliban's reintegration into the drug trade, and are strengthening it politically. In 2001 and 2002, Operation Enduring Freedom not only deposed the Taliban from power, but also pushed it out of the Afghan opium economy that it had sponsored and taxed for many years. On the run and hiding in Pakistan, the Taliban was not able to perform the security and regulatory functions for the opium economy that it used to. Poppy cultivation rebounded to pre-2000 levels of about 3,000 mt a year.

After the failure of a compensated eradication scheme in 2003, counternarcotics efforts shifted to beefed-up interdiction and uncompensated eradication. Conducted by local Afghan officials, interdiction efforts frequently targeted vulnerable small traders as well as competition, while increasing the profits of those who carried out interdiction. The result has been the vertical integration of the industry, and the rise of prominent drug dealers with political power.[8] At the same time, interdiction has created the need for new kind of protection, and the targeted traffickers frequently hire the Taliban to shield them against the state and drug competition.

Whereas interdiction created an opening for the Taliban with the traffickers, forced eradication gave the Taliban new access to the population. Endorsed in the August 2007 *U.S. Counternarcotics Strategy Report for*

Afghanistan[9] as the essential mechanism to suppress poppy cultivation, eradication counterproductively strengthens the Taliban politically in multiple ways. The impoverished population continues to be critically dependent on the opium economy for its basic livelihood, and eradication thus alienates them from the state, and from the local officials and tribal elites who implement it. Eradication allows the Taliban to provide security and regulatory services to the population by protecting their poppy fields.[10] Eradication thus cements the bond between the population and the Taliban, motivating the population not to provide intelligence on the Taliban to NATO and government units. Finally, by driving them further into debt and eliminating their livelihood, eradication also displaces the population, and physically drives them into the hands of the Taliban.

Hailed as a major success, the 2005 eradication campaign in Nangarhar is a case in point. Through promises of alternative developments and threats of imprisonment, cultivation in Nangarhar was dramatically decreased, a crucial contribution to a 21% reduction in the area of cultivation countrywide. But the promises of alternative livelihoods never materialized for many. Cash-for-work programs reached only a small percentage of the rural population, and the pauperization of the population in Nangarhar was devastating.[11] Unable to repay debts, farmers were forced to sell their daughters as young as three or abscond to Pakistan, where many refilled the ranks of the Taliban. Also, alternative livelihoods programs at the national level so far have failed to address the structural drivers of opium cultivation, including failing to provide access to legal microcredit and to facilitate land rent without the need to cultivate opium poppy. Much of the rural population still depends on the cultivation of opium for microcredit and to rent land.[12] The Nangarhar "success" was neither sustained (production skyrocketed in 2009) nor sustainable.[13] Moreover, Nangarhar became another critical epicenter of insurgency, in addition to Helmand, Kandahar, and Uruzgan.

There is an inherent time lag between eradication and creating alternative livelihoods. Eradication in a particular locale can be carried out almost overnight, but establishing a legal sustainable economy that provides sufficient employment takes years. Without prior well-funded and extensive efforts at building a legal economy, eradication thus results in disillusionment, unrest, and failure.

Indeed, the 2008 and 2009 poppy suppression campaigns in Nangarhar further show both the unsustainable and counterproductive nature of premature measures. After poppy shot up to pre-eradication levels in Nangarhar in 2007, new governor Gul Agha Shirzai—a presidential hopeful and a prominent tribal leader from Kandahar province—was determined to suppress cultivation to score political points with the international community, and with Kabul for his presidential candidacy. As a result of his suppression efforts—including bans on cultivation, forced eradication, imprisonment of violators, and claims that NATO would bomb the houses of those who cultivate poppy or keep opium—cultivation went down to almost zero. This has been hailed as a major success to be emulated throughout Afghanistan.

In fact, like the 2005 ban, the 2008-09 ban impoverished many, often causing household incomes to fall 90%, and driving much of the population into debt. As before, legal economic activities failed to materialize, especially for those further away from the capital of Jalalabad. Many coped with economic deprivation by resorting to crime, such as kidnapping and robberies; others, by seeking employment in the poppy fields of Helmand; and still others by migrating to Pakistan, where they frequently ended up recruited by the Taliban. The population became deeply alienated from the government, resorting to strikes and attacks on government forces, and districts that were severely economically hit—such as Khogiani, Achin, and Shinwar—have become no-go zones for the Afghan government and NGOs. Although those tribal areas have historically been opposed to the Taliban, Taliban mobilization there has taken off to an unprecedented degree. The populations began allowing the Taliban to cross over from Pakistan, and intelligence provision to Afghan forces and NATO has almost dried up. Tribal elders who supported the ban became discredited, and the collapse of their legitimacy is providing an opportunity for the Taliban to insert itself into the decision-making structures in those areas.[14] Overall, even "successful" poppy suppression did not bankrupt the insurgency or reduce instability and violence. Just the opposite: it fueled both.

After years of such inappropriate focus on eradication of the poppy crop, the new counternarcotics strategy for Afghanistan, announced by U.S. government officials in summer 2009, promises to mesh well with the counterinsurgency and state-building effort. By scaling back eradication and emphasizing interdiction and development, it will help separate the population from the Taliban. If designed well, the interdiction effort can also contribute to establishing rule of law in Afghanistan and reducing the power of criminal groups, Taliban-linked or not. But there should be little expectation that the new interdiction effort can significantly constrain Taliban income, which comes from many sources other than drugs, including taxation of economic activity, illicit logging, illicit trade in gems and wildlife, and fundraising in Pakistan and the Middle East.[15]

On its own, a well-designed counternarcotics policy is not sufficient for success in Afghanistan. But it is indispensible.

IF SUCCESS, THEN WHAT?

Let's imagine that eradication could somehow miraculously and rapidly wipe out opium cultivation in Afghanistan, and the campaign was executed in such a way that made replanting within the country impossible. For example, assume that despite the controversy about resorting to "biological warfare" and its potential negative effects on other crops, animals, and human health, a mycoherbicide was sprayed throughout the country and persisted in the soil for several years, destroying any poppy seeds that farmers attempted to plant. (Currently Kabul opposes any such spraying with any agent.)

Immediately, Afghanistan's GDP would be slashed by at least thirty percent, deepening the economic crisis of the very poor rural population. Without comprehensive economic development that addresses all structural drivers of illicit crop cultivation and licit crop underdevelopment, legal subsistence crops would struggle and potentially experience massive failures due to a lack of irrigation systems and fertilizers. Even wheat—intensively pushed since 2008 as the replacement crop in Afghanistan because of an unusually favorable (and unsustainable) wheat-to-opium price ratio—would fail to offset the individual income losses and the macroeconomic dislocation effects. Not only does the wheat program fail to address the multiple and complex drivers of opium poppy cultivation,[16] but also most farmers do not have access to enough land to generate even necessary subsistence out of wheat. Moreover, as wheat is far less labor-intensive than opium poppy, even a wholesale replacement of the entire area currently cultivated with poppy by wheat would generate a massive rise in unemployment.

Without robust and multifaceted development, forced poppy suppression would mean that farmers would not be able to obtain microcredit, access to land, and productive assets, thus becoming further indebted. Even in cities, much economic activity, such as construction and trade with durables, would greatly decrease, since these economic activities are now massively underwritten by drug money. Social strife and chaos would ensue, as well as massive migration to Pakistan. The Taliban insurgency would be strengthened.

But apart from these economic, political, and military effects, which are magnified consequences of any eradication that targets the rural poor without providing them with immediate and reliable access to legal alternatives, two other critical questions need to be asked regarding the "what then." First, what illicit economy would replace the existing opium one in Afghanistan? And second, to what country would opium production shift?

Illicit economies rarely simply disappear. A large illicit economy not only satisfies the socioeconomic needs of the population, but also generates widespread smuggling knowhow, extensive criminal networks, and numerous powerful actors with vested interests in the preservation of an illicit economy. These actors include criminal and belligerent groups, corrupt government officials, and political powerbrokers. This infrastructure of crime can easily be transferred from one illicit economy to another. In Colombia, the drug trade built on several decades of smuggling with cigarettes, household goods, marijuana and emeralds. Many of the original smugglers emerged as prominent Colombian drug capos.[17] In Myanmar, the eradication of opium poppy since the late 1990s (crucially helped by overproduction in Afghanistan) gave rise to an extensive production of methamphetamines, rampant illicit logging, and a massive increase in the illegal trade of wildlife.[18] In Afghanistan itself, the illegal drug economy had built on decades of smuggling of various sorts, including a very large illicit traffic of licit goods.

In Afghanistan, the least dangerous and potentially most easily suppressible illicit replacement economy would be just such an increase in this illicit trade of licit goods. This traffic exists as a result of the Afghan Transit Trade Agreement, under which goods can be imported to Pakistan duty-free for re-export into Afghanistan. Goods billed for Afghanistan, arriving, for example, from Dubai, are then smuggled back from Afghanistan into Pakistan where both traders and consumers avoid having to pay customs. Although profits from the illicit traffic (at times over $1 billion per year)[19] could rival those from drugs, if Pakistan and Afghanistan set their tariffs at the same level, this trade would disappear. Already today, as in the 1990s, the trade generates extensive revenues for the Taliban and others.

A considerably more ominous illicit replacement economy would be the production of synthetic drugs, such as methamphetamines. Afghanistan would of course face stiff competition from Myanmar, Thailand, and Mexico, but the global market for synthetic drugs is rapidly growing; Afghanistan would likely be able to cut in on it. In that case, Afghanistan would still suffer from the same political, economic, and social vices of illegal drug production. But the rural population would now be left destitute since the production of synthetic drugs is less labor-intensive than the cultivation of opium, and hence could employ only a tiny fraction of the farmers and laborers of the opium economy. At the same time, large traffickers, corrupt government officials, and belligerent groups could easily maintain the level of income they have been obtaining from the opium economy. One effect of the lower labor-intensiveness of synthetic drug production would be a further tightening of control over the economy into the hands of few individuals, with a corresponding rise in their political influence. Moreover, the production of synthetic drugs would be considerably harder to detect and disrupt. Two other illicit economies already in existence in Afghanistan—illicit logging and wildlife smuggling—would be strengthened, further contributing to environmental and economic destruction of the countryside through soil erosion, overgrazing, and changes to water level.

THE GOLDEN TRIANGLE'S UNLIKELY NEW HIGH

The second what-then question of vital importance for the United States is to what country opium cultivation would shift. Given high world demand for illicit opiates, suppression of poppy cultivation in Afghanistan would not leave a highly lucrative market unsatiated, but would shift it elsewhere.

Afghanistan itself first became a significant opium producer as a result of suppression policies and acts of nature elsewhere. Some level of opium poppy cultivation took place in Afghanistan for centuries, and in fact frustrated British counterinsurgency efforts during the 19th century and critically influenced state-building efforts in Afghanistan during the same period.[20] But it was only in the mid-1950s, after poppy cultivation was banned in neighboring Iran, that Afghanistan really burst onto the international drug scene and became a place for Western hippies to "turn on, tune in, and drop out" inexpensively. Initially Iran was Afghanistan's principal market, but in the mid-1970s, when Western demand for heroin greatly expanded and political instability and a prolonged drought disrupted the flow of drugs from Southeast Asia's Golden Triangle, Afghanistan began to supply large quantities of illicit opiates to the global market.[21]

Just as in the 1950s and 1980s, poppy suppression in Afghanistan in the absence of a reduction in the global demand for opiates would simply shift cultivation to another locale. Unlike coca, whose cultivation is more geographically limited by climate requirements, poppy can be cultivated in most of the world. Nonetheless, there are three likely candidates for a large-scale poppy cultivation relocation from Afghanistan.

From a U.S. strategic perspective, the most optimistic scenario would be an increase in opium cultivation in the Golden Triangle, specifically Burma. Recent production suppression there has left the ethnic populations in the hill periphery regions, such as the Wa, destitute.[22] Although the ethnic elites—former rebels and now leaders of their semiautonomous regions—are cooking Ecstasy, large segments of their populations have food security for only eight months a year, relying on UN food aid for the remaining four. Critical poverty, disease, addiction, and outmigration are widespread—as are coping mechanisms such as illicit logging, trade in wildlife, and foraging in forests.[23] The immiseration of the ethnic groups at the hands of both the regime in Naypyidaw and their local leadership has antagonized the population. Although they have no love for the abusive and discriminatory central government, after decades of war and now over ten years of economic deprivation as a result of poppy suppression in the absence of legal alternatives, they also have little commitment to their ethnic leaders and local representatives. One manifestation of this weakening of the bond between the ethnic populations and the ethnic-insurgent leaders who control the territories has been the resounding defeat of the ethnic groups by the junta's forces during the flare-up of the country's ethnic conflict in the summer and fall of 2009. The rebels' defeats have many sources, including the strengthening of the junta's military forces over the past fifteen years even as the rebel armies have become weakened and demobilized to some extent, the fractious nature of the anti-central-government alliances, and the high levels of internal infighting.[24] But the failure of the groups' leaders to mobilize the population even as the junta pushes for elections and referenda in 2010 threatens to further constrict the autonomy of the ethnic groups.

If opium production returned to Burma, the immediate economic crisis would be somewhat lessened, even though the illegal narcotics economy creates its own trap of poverty and abuse. Both the central junta and the various now largely-disarmed rebel groups would again tap into the re-emergent opium economy,[25] and would increase their physical resources and domestic political capital since they could provide livelihood for their populations. Thus violent conflict between the central junta and ethnic insurgencies may intensify.

The strengthening of the junta and of the demobilized rebel groups would be adverse to U.S. interests in democracy and human rights—all the more painful after the junta's brutalization of protesting Buddhist monks in fall 2007.[26] It would not however pose a direct threat to U.S. security. Although they would be further weakened in effectiveness, U.S. sanctions on Myanmar for human rights violations are already critically undermined by China's, India's, and Thailand's trade with the country. An increase in cultivation may further complicate the new U.S. effort to couple sanctions against the junta with a cautious engagement with the regime that the Obama administration began cautiously trying out in the fall of 2009;[27] but poppy suppression undertaken by the junta during the Clinton and Bush administrations did not ease the U.S.-Myanmar relationship or domestic oppression in the country.

China would be unhappy with the rise in Burma's production of opiates. As in the 1990s, it would likely pressure the junta and the various ethnic groups to eradicate the poppy fields, both to arrest the increasing rate of addiction in China and to limit the power of Chinese crime organizations, many of which are closely linked to Burmese illicit economies. These crime organizations are undermining the centrality of power of the Chinese Communist Party in the periphery.

Despite having the least negative impact on U.S. strategic interests, this scenario where the bulk of opiate production shifts to Burma is not likely to materialize. Although some increase in production in Burma would take place, a wholesale transfer of Afghanistan's opium economy is unlikely. First, because of climatic and soil conditions, Burmese opium has smaller yields and is of lesser quality (i.e., has less morphine content) than Afghan/Central Asian opium. Second, important current heroin refining infrastructure and smuggling routes are now located in the territory of Afghanistan's neighbors.

CENTRAL ASIA: GETTING HOOKED

Under a second scenario, opium cultivation and production would shift to Central Asia's former Soviet republics. These countries have already become key smuggling routes for opium and heroin from Afghanistan to Russia and Turkey, and on to the rest of Europe. Many Afghan heroin laboratories have emerged on the border with Tajikistan, Uzbekistan, and Turkmenistan. These countries' border interdiction capabilities remain critically limited, with border patrol officials frequently on the payroll of drug traffickers.[28] Government corruption is widespread, and counternarcotics efforts are frequently manipulated to placate the United States, eliminate drug competition, and crack down against domestic political opposition. All of these countries have experienced a rampant increase in drug addiction rates, driven by both the ready availability of opiates and widespread poverty, including some of the worst living standards within the Commonwealth of Independent States (CIS). Apart from weak and corrupt law enforcement, climatic and soil conditions for cultivation in the Central Asia region are ideal for the production of the illicit crops. During the 1990s, illicit cultivation of both opium poppy and cannabis gradually emerged in many CIS countries.[29] Already during the 1990s civil war in Tajikistan, the drug trade was almost the sole economic activity of the Gorno Badakshan region, and spread to other parts of the country as well.[30]

Large-scale cultivation in the region poses at least three dangers for the United States. The first is the emergence in CIS countries of a jihadist hub with access to drug profits. Since the demise of Afghanistan as a safe haven, many jihadists from Central Asia and the Middle East have been looking for a new base. Although the tribal territories of Pakistan are already pulling in jihadist terrorists, the shift of poppy cultivation to CIS countries would serve as a great magnet, with vast money to be obtained for jihad.

During the 1990s, the Islamic Movement of Uzbekistan (IMU) already profited from the Afghan drug trade, emerging as a major courier organization in the region. Motivated by religious extremism, it carried out military operations in Tajikistan, Uzbekistan, and Kyrgyzstan.[31] Although the group never posed a serious threat to regional governments, it developed networks interlocking with those of other militant Islamic groups, including the Taliban and al-Qaeda, and in fact absorbed extremist Arabs, Chechens, Dagestanis, Uighurs, and ex-Iraqi jihadists in Pakistan. It has since developed networks in Europe.[32] Since 2004, it has been present and active in Pakistan, especially in South Waziristan, fueling the Salafi insurgency there.

With opium production shifting to CIS countries, both law enforcement against the drug trade and efforts against the jihadists would become more difficult for the U.S. to conduct since it would not have the same military and intelligence assets there that it now has in Afghanistan. Apart from sensitive clandestine operations and strikes from air and other remote platforms, it would have to rely on regional governments for action against terrorists and against drugs. The U.S. would thus exercise much less control over policy against the drug-terror nexus in the region than it can in Afghanistan.

The second danger would be official crackdowns on Islam and Islamists in Central Asia disguised as counternarcotics policy. Local governments' heavy-handed measures against Islamists and other domestic opponents, while billed as crackdowns against the drug trade, would increase instability in the region and further radicalize the poor population grappling with its post-Soviet Communist and repressed Islamic identity. Already it has become common practice in the region to accuse political enemies of being drug dealers. Counternarcotics measures would also alienate the population from their governments and from the U.S. Unlike in Latin America, the balloon effect in Central Asia would involve not only a shift of drug production to a new area, but also the spread of antagonism against the United States among populations on the brink of falling into the hands of anti-U.S. Islamists.

Finally, a shift of opium poppy cultivation to Central Asia may jeopardize U.S. oil interests in the region. With around 50 billion barrels of oil at stake,[33] the U.S., Russia, China, and Iran have become involved in intense competition over the region's potential resources. Large-scale opium cultivation in the CIS countries would be destabilizing—further increasing crime and terrorist presence, and thus jeopardizing potential economic investment and trade. China has an additional interest in preventing the spread of opium cultivation to the Xinjiang province, which would provide the rebellious Uighurs with access to drug profits and political capital. Instability would also increase as a result of repressive counterdrug policies, again complicating oil exploitation. Politically-sensitive counternarcotics operations would increase mutual blame among the Caspian countries for the drug problem, further weakening their already minimal cooperation.

PAKISTAN: DRUGS, TRIBES, AND SALAFISTS

By far the worst scenario from the U.S. strategic perspective would be the shift of poppy cultivation to the Federally Administered Tribal Areas (FATA), the North-West Frontier Province (NWFP), or even Pakistan's Punjab province. For over twenty years, Pakistan has been a major heroin refining and smuggling hub. It has an extensive *hawala* system that has been used for moving drug profits. Today, these territories also have extensive and well-organized Salafi insurgent and terrorist groups that seek to limit the reach of the Pakistani state and topple Pakistan's government. A relocation of poppy cultivation there would be highly detrimental to U.S. interests, since it would contribute to a critical undermining of the Pakistani state and fuel jihadist insurgency. Such a shift would not only increase profit possibilities for Pakistani belligerents, but also provide them with significant political capital by allowing them to become significant local employers: FATA, NWFP, Baluchistan, and Punjab are all areas with minimal employment opportunities.

Nor is Pakistan a newcomer to the drug trade. Pakistan's history of opium production dates back to the British Raj, when opium was produced legally and sold to opium dens first in Britain and later in China. Unlike postcolonial India, Pakistan was not able to maintain the International Narcotics Control Board (INCB) license for legal production of medical opiates, such as morphine, because it was unable to comply with such INCB rules as preventing diversion to the illicit trade. As a result, opium poppy cultivation became illegal in Pakistan in the 1970s.

During the heyday of illicit poppy cultivation in Pakistan in the 1980s, opium poppy was grown in the FATA and NFWP, with agencies such as Bannu, Khyber, and Dir being significant loci of cultivation. In many of these highly isolated areas, opium poppy cultivation involved entire tribes and represented the bulk of the local economy.[34] Pakistan was also the locus of heroin production and smuggling, with prominent official actors such as Pakistan's military and Inter-Services Intelligence agency (ISI) deeply involved in the heroin trade. During the Zia ul-Haq era, drug-related corruption in Pakistan reached the highest levels of government, including close Zia associates such as NWFP governor General Fazle Haq.[35]

Throughout the 1980s, Pakistan's opiate production surpassed Afghanistan's, and for at least brief periods Pakistan was the world's number one producer of illicit opiates.[36] In retrospect, Pakistan's peak production of 800 metric tons is paltry compared to Afghanistan's 8,000. But U.S.-sponsored eradication in the area during the 1980s generated violent protests and political difficulties.[37] Eradication efforts proved unsustainable even for Zia's military dictatorship.

In the 1990s, emphasis was thus placed on generating legal alternatives to wean Pakistani tribes from economic reliance on drugs. Consisting mainly of small rural infrastructure projects and special economic opportunity zones (similar to those for textiles promoted by the current U.S. administration in Pakistan), alternative development efforts in Pakistan's drug producing areas in the 1990s brought many benefits to both the local economy and the Pakistani state.[38] They better linked isolated areas with the rest of Pakistan, and increased local populations' identification with Pakistan. Until these development efforts in the 1990s, many in FATA never identified themselves as Pakistani: their identification was often tribe-based, frequently in direct opposition to the Pakistani state. The 1990s' alternative development efforts also beefed up the weakening legitimacy of local political elites and pro-Islamabad political agents, although these powerbrokers frequently engaged in counternarcotics efforts and rural development with the purpose of manipulating these efforts to shore up their political capital with various and varied local groups; they did not necessarily see full and lasting suppression of poppy in their areas as in their interest. Anticipating that if poppy altogether disappeared from their areas, so would economic aid and rural development efforts, political agents and tribal khans frequently sought to perpetuate some level of cultivation to both appease their constituencies and to assure a continuing stream of aid.

In 2002, UNODC declared Pakistan cultivation-free. However, the dominant reason for the decline in opium poppy cultivation in Pakistan was not counternarcotics efforts—whether eradication or alternative development—but rather the wholesale shift of cultivation to Afghanistan during the 1990s. Pakistani trafficking networks frequently remained undiminished by the shift, and higher-value sectors of the drug industry have continue to be located in Peshawar and elsewhere in Pakistan.

Moreover, the positive political and economic effects of alternative development efforts in Pakistan in the 1990s frequently proved ephemeral as these alternative livelihood efforts failed to generate sustainable employment. Many have continued to be consigned to subsistence agriculture, trucking and smuggling, or to migration, including to other parts of Pakistan or to Dubai.[39] Despite their limited effectiveness, the alternative development efforts were still far less politically destabilizing than previous poppy eradication drives in Pakistan in the late 1980s and early 1990s.

The extensive drug-trade network, the history of poppy cultivation, and the poor central-government control over the border regions with Afghanistan make Pakistan a likely candidate for vastly increased poppy cultivation if Afghan production were disrupted. Already, some opium cultivation has emerged in Baluchistan, Khyber, Kohistan, and Kala Dhaka. Given the lack of systematic drug surveys in those and other areas of Pakistan, the extent of cultivation there is difficult to gauge, but some assessments report a resurgence of cultivation up to 2000 hectares in recent years. (It may well be more, given the lack of economic alternatives in the area, the history of opium poppy cultivation there, and the fact that the level of poppy cultivation in Kashmir on both sides of the Line of Control is estimated at 8000 hectares.)[40]

The fluid cross-border movement of the population, whether Afghan or Pakistani Taliban or others, would facilitate such a relocation of production. Afghan refugees and mujahidin in Pakistan during the 1980s were a conduit for the spread of cultivation to Afghanistan.[41] Today, another out-migration from Afghanistan, whether caused by the Taliban insurgency or economic displacement due to massive eradication, would facilitate the shift of cultivation to Pakistan.

There is little evidence that today either the Afghan Taliban or the Pakistani Taliban (including Tehrik-i-Taliban and Tehrik-e-Nifaz-e-Sharia-e-Mohammadi) has systematically penetrated the slightly resurgent opium poppy cultivation in FATA and NWFP, even though they may have penetrated trafficking in drugs and precursor agents in Pakistan. Instead, it appears that the main sources of the Pakistani Taliban's income include smuggling in legal goods; charging tolls and protection fees; taxation of all economic activity in the areas they operate (some being highly profitable, such as marble mining); theft and resale of NATO supplies heading to Afghanistan via Pakistan; illicit logging; and fundraising in Pakistan the broader Middle East.[42] While profits from such a diverse portfolio of activities can equal or even surpass profits from drugs, their main downside—from the perspective of belligerent actors—is that these economic activities are not labor-intensive. Jihadi groups undertaking these activities in Pakistan cannot present themselves as large-scale providers of employment to the local population, unlike when they sponsor the highly labor-intensive cultivation of opium poppy.

If extensive poppy cultivation shifted to Pakistan, the consequences for U.S. national security would be serious. FATA and even parts of NWFP are already hubs for anti-American jihadists, as the jihadi takeover of Swat and Malakand in spring 2009 revealed. Salafi insurgent and global terrorist networks have been taking root in southern Punjab, and go beyond Lashkar-e-Taiba's presence there.

Not only could al-Qaeda and affiliated terrorist groups profit financially from drug trafficking and money laundering, but ready access to cultivation (which these groups, unlike the Taliban, do not have as long as cultivation is centered in Afghanistan) would allow them to provide a superior livelihood to vastly undeveloped regions in Pakistan, and thus obtain significant political capital.

If production shifted to Pakistan, the sponsorship of cultivation would allow these groups to distribute significant economic benefits to the population, a key source of legitimacy. Just like in Afghanistan in the 1980s, the jihadists would thus be able to outperform traditional tribal elites in providing for the population's needs. One of the greatest threats to al-Qaeda and affiliate jihadi groups in Pakistan paradoxically comes from their aggressive attacks against the tribal leadership in Waziristan. The sponsorship of relocated opium cultivation would allow the jihadists to offset the potential losses of support resulting from attacks on the tribal elite. In short, a shift of cultivation to Pakistan would greatly enhance the ability of al-Qaeda and other jihadist terrorist groups to consolidate their presence in Pakistan's tribal areas.

If opium poppy cultivation again shifted to Pakistan on a large scale, Pakistan would find it far more difficult to mount effective counternarcotics measures. Given the hollowing out of the Pakistani state, the multifaceted collapse of its administrative capacity in FATA and NWFP, and the overall macroeconomic crisis of the country (which is acutely felt in FATA and NWFP), the state would find it difficult to develop sufficient legal employment opportunities. The area could easily become not only fully alienated from the central government, but also economically independent from it.

Government efforts at eradication would generate protests and uprisings, cementing the bond between the jihadists and the population, and weakening Islamabad's already tenuous legitimacy. Weak central government presence there (military and otherwise) would compromise counternarcotics efforts, but eradication would greatly undermine even modest counterterrorism and stabilization efforts by Islamabad. The depletion of the political capital of both Pakistan's civilian elites and its military over the 1990s and 2000s would further make any forced eradication far more politically costly and difficult to sustain. Given the existence of belligerency in the likely poppy-growing regions, forced eradication would greatly fuel militancy and generate far greater negative security externalities than it did in the 1980s and early 1990s—when social protest had not congealed into a highly organized form, social networks were not premobilized, and pernicious political entrepreneurs were not at the ready to capitalize on social discontent.

Because of the continuing geographic, political, and social isolation of these areas, the lack of rule of law and the paucity of productive assets—both physical resources and human capital—generating employment opportunities in those areas will be highly challenging under the best of circumstances.

Current development efforts in FATA and NWFP sponsored by the United States, including those provided by the Kerry-Lugar Bill of 2009, thus need to take advantage of the fact that they do not face competition from an entrenched labor-intensive illicit economy: the existing illicit economies in those areas, primarily smuggling, are not labor intensive. At the same time, it is imperative to advance and intensify current development efforts as much as possible and direct them toward sustainable job creation (not simply temporary employment in short-term small-scale rural infrastructure building) to prepare for having to mitigate the social, economic, and political effects of any extensive relocation of opium poppy cultivation to the area in the future.

A large-scale shift of opium poppy cultivation to Pakistan in the near and medium-term would thus contribute to a further critical weakening of the state and undermine its control of and even reach to some of the areas in Pakistan most susceptible to jihadism. Such a large-scale shift of cultivation would also likely leak into Baluchistan, where heroin processing facilities and trafficking networks are already extensively present. It would thus enable Baluchi nationalists to tap into the drug economy and strengthen the Baluchi insurgency in a multiple way, thus further threatening the territorial integrity of Pakistan and diverting the state's attention from the jihadi threat. Assisting the government of Pakistan today to the extent possible in both rural development efforts and in enhancing the effectiveness of its interdiction and law enforcement capacity has the potential to reduce possible security and political threats should such a relocation take place.

WHAT CAN BE DONE IN AFGHANISTAN AND THE BROADER REGION

A counternarcotics policy in Afghanistan (as elsewhere) must be cognizant not only of the economic, political, and security effects within the country itself, but also of its broader ramifications. The policy must take into the account the economic roles opium plays in Afghanistan, as well as the way counternarcotics policies have become a political weapon for the Taliban.

Eradication can be a part of broad counternarcotics packages that integrate security, rural development, governance, and state-building. But it should be limited to areas where the Taliban does not have a reach, and only against those who have assured legal livelihood alternatives. At the same time, care needs to be taken that such "smart eradication" is not misconstrued as tribal and ethnic discrimination.

At the same time, NATO and Kabul cannot rely on counternarcotics measures to degrade the Taliban's physical resources. The Taliban can only be weakened physically if the coalition and Afghan forces increase their own military assets devoted to counterinsurgency. The Taliban's safe havens in Pakistan also need to be addressed.

Economic development must be brought to locales where the Taliban is active. No progress against narcotics can be lasting and without negative repercussions unless integrated with prior rural development. In the Pashtun belt, this cannot be achieved until the Taliban is defeated. Without consistent security against Taliban attacks, economic projects will fall apart, the population will not be able to take advantage of them, and investments will not be viable.

But the need for security as a precursor to sustainable development should not be used as an excuse to postpone all economic projects. Unless at least some immediate economic improvements are brought rapidly to the population in contested areas, counterinsurgency efforts cannot win hearts and minds. In the short term, the population must receive security improvements combined with a fast injection of visible economic aid, followed in the longer term by comprehensive, sustained, and well-funded economic development throughout the country.

Rural development needs to address all structural drivers of poppy cultivation. It needs to focus not only on the farm, but also on value-added chains and assured markets. It needs to emphasize diversified high-value, labor intensive crops, and not center on wheat.

Top drug traffickers in important positions of power should gradually be removed, to limit their political power if not to cripple the drug industry. But actions against them need to be ethnically balanced, and should be undertaken only once beefed-up police forces are in place to deal with the high potential of wars among the remaining traffickers over control of the industry—and also against the state. (Colombia during the 1980s and 1990s and Mexico today provide vivid examples of the debilitating effects of such drugs wars, and the state's inability to cope with them.)

Interdiction needs to focus on reducing the coercive and corrupting power of crime groups. Before interdiction measures are undertaken, an analysis of second- and third-order effects needs to be conducted. It needs to be carefully calibrated with the strength of law enforcement in Afghanistan to avoid provoking dangerous turf wars, ethnic violence, and cementing the relationship between the Taliban and the traffickers. It also needs to target top traffickers linked to the Afghan government. Interdiction needs to encompass building the justice and corrections system in Afghanistan and broad rule of law efforts.

Reforming Afghanistan's law enforcement is vital. The key metrics, though, should not be the number of interdiction raids and hectares eradicated, but rather the extent of security the police bring to the area and the growing confidence of the population that, overall, the police represent an impartial, honest, and competent organ of the state—and not predatory warlords dressed in state uniforms. Although such metrics are considerably more difficult to measure than the current simplistic ones, obtaining such information is possible if intelligence officers and development workers focus on collecting it. Such metrics will result in considerably more accurate and useful assessments of policy effectiveness.[43]

At the regional level, the United States should build cooperation among Afghanistan's neighbors, and help them develop economically. This will hinge on the geopolitical situation in Central Asia unrelated to narcotics, but the U.S. should nonetheless nudge regional governments to move beyond declarative cooperation in counternarcotics to action, at least on border security and intelligence sharing. The U.S., China, and Russia have much to gain from cooperating in combating narcotics in Central Asia, which if done wisely could lead to state-building and economic development of the region.

Moving Pakistan to serious cooperation on counternarcotics should production shift there will be a tall task as long as Islamabad continues to exercise only weak control over the regions where cultivation would likely take place. Accusations of sovereignty violations, similar to those that arose with respect to Kerry-Lugar, are easily exploitable by the political opposition to the government; the fact that a ready audience exists among the alienated population will make any such visible cooperation difficult and possibly counterproductive for other U.S. other interests. Thus, the best counternarcotics policy with respect to Pakistan is to foster state-building and help Islamabad to extend security and economic development to disaffected border areas. This includes quiet and below-the-radar counterinsurgency assistance, but also assistance in developing holding forces and police and law enforcement capacity, and advancing the rule of law.

Making a major push on economic development of Pakistan's many marginalized areas is no easy task, and needs to have local Pakistani ownership. But however difficult and complex, it needs to be intensified as much as possible and as much as the security situation permits before large-scale poppy cultivation shifts there.

In both Afghanistan and Pakistan, priority needs to be given to efforts to improve governance at the national and local levels. But the international community cannot define governance simply as reducing the numbers of hectares of poppy eradicated. Good governance must be understood as the ability of local governing authorities to improve the lives of the people, as well as doing so within the context of law. Thus prematurely banning or eradicating poppy will only cause the immiseration of the population the governing authorities are supposed to be helping—and hence will create profound doubts about their accountability to, and usefulness for, the people.

Such an undertaking in Pakistan and Central Asia will take many years, despite the recent injection of U.S. funds for the project. A rapid shift of widespread opium cultivation to these countries would leave them unprepared to cope with the associated problems, and jeopardize U.S. strategic interests in the area.

At the global level, demand-reduction efforts need to be elevated from a political afterthought to the core pillar of U.S. counternarcotics policies. The Obama administration must put the money where its mouth is. Demand-reduction measures must contain both treatment and prevention components. Moreover, demand-reduction efforts must be worldwide, not simply directed at U.S. or Western consumption. The non-Western world has become a major consumer of illicit drugs, with Brazil, Pakistan, Iran, Russia, and China constituting strong secondary markets. Instead of simply exporting drug suppression policies, the United States should also help governments in these countries reduce addiction rates. Moreover, demand-reduction efforts should focus on multiple drugs, including synthetics. With significantly weaker global demand, suppression efforts would be not only more manageable, but their negative political and geostrategic repercussions would also be reduced.

ENDNOTES

1 Special envoy for Afghanistan and Pakistan Richard Holbrooke announced the new policy in various international forums in the spring and summer of 2009. See Rachel Donadio, "New Course of Antidrug Efforts in Afghanistan," *New York Times,* June 27, 2009.

2 United Nations Office on Drugs and Crime (UNODC), *Afghanistan Opium Survey 2007,* Aug. 2007, p. iv; author's interview with UNODC officials specializing in the Afghan and European market, Geneva, Nov. 2007.

3 UNODC, *Afghanistan Opium Survey 2009*, Sept. 2009.

4 Ibid.

5 For years, this demand was believed to be at approximately 3,000 mt a year. After several years of opium production in Afghanistan doubly or triply surpassing the estimated total global demand, UNODC this year increased the total global demand estimate to 5,000 mt. Whether the actual level is 3,000 mt, 5,000 mt, or some other figure, it is quite likely that the multi-year overproduction in Afghanistan has resulted in significant stockpiles of either opium or heroin.

6 Since 2002, the percentage of drugs to licit GDP has oscillated between 60 and 30 percent, not because the illicit economy has been reduced, but due to the expansion of some sectors of the legal economy, such as telecommunications. The latest estimate was reported to the author by a World Bank official. Confusion about exact percentages partially stems from whether estimates use licit GDP or overall GDP as a baseline, and partially from the extraordinary difficulties in estimating the size of an illegal economy; in the case of Afghanistan, even the size of the legal economy is difficult to estimate, since much of it is informal. Thus, even UNODC does not consistently report this percentage every year. For a previous high estimate, see, for example, United Nations Office on Drugs and Crime, "Opium Amounts to Half of Afghanistan's GDP in 2007, Reports UNODC," Nov. 16, 2007.

7 Gen. Stanley McChrystal, *COMISAF's Initial Assessment*, Aug. 30, 2009.

8 See Adam Pain, "Opium Trading Systems in Helmand and Ghor Provinces," in *Afghanistan's Drug Industry* (Vienna and Washington, DC: UNODC and World Bank, Doris Buddenberg & William Byrd, eds., 2006), pp. 77-115; Mark Shaw, "Drug Trafficking and the Development of Organized Crime in Post-Taliban Afghanistan," *Afghanistan's Drug Industry* (Vienna and Washington, DC: UNODC and World Bank, Doris Buddenberg & William Byrd, eds., 2006), pp. 189-214.

9 Thomas A. Schweich, *U.S. Counternarcotics Strategy for Afghanistan*, Aug. 2007.

10 For a history of such Taliban protection, see Vanda Felbab-Brown, "Afghanistan: When Counternarcotics Undermine Counterterrorism," *Washington Quarterly*, Fall 2005, pp. 55-72

11 David Manfield, "Pariah or Poverty?: The Opium Ban in the Province Nangarhar in 2004/05 Growing Season and Its Impact on Rural Livelihood Strategies," GTZ Policy Brief No. 1, Sept. 2005.

12 For the slow progress of alternative livelihoods and the hampering effect of insecurity, see Joel Hafvenstein, *Opium Season* (Lyons Press, 2007).

13 UNODC, *Afghanistan Opium Survey 2007*.

14 Author's interviews with U.S. and NATO intelligence officers deployed to Nangarhar, and with alternative development consultants working in Nangarhar, Washington, DC, spring and summer 2009.

15 For details on the new counternarcotics policy and its promise as well as potential pitfalls and false expectations, see Vanda Felbab-Brown, "The Obama Administration's New Counternarcotics Policy in Afghanistan: Its Promises and Potential Pitfalls," *Brookings Policy Brief Series*, No. 171, Sept. 2009.

16 David Mansfield, "The Economic Superiority of Illicit Drug Production: Myth and Reality—Opium Poppy Cultivation in Afghanistan," paper prepared for the

International Conference on Alternative Development in Drug Control and Cooperation, Feldafing, Germany, Aug. 2001.

[17] Francisco Thoumi, *Illegal Drugs, Economy, and Society in the Andes* (Baltimore: John Hopkins University Press, 2003).

[18] For the evolution of Myanmar's illicit economies, including the drug trade, see Jake Sherman, "Burma: Lessons from Cease-Fires," in *The Political Economy of Armed Conflict: Beyond Greed and Grievance* (Boulder: Lynne Rienner Publishers, Karen Ballentine & Jake Sherman eds., 2003), pp. 225-258; see also chapter 6 of Vanda Felbab-Brown, *Shooting Up: Counterinsurgency and the War on Drugs* (Washington, DC: Brookings Institution Press, 2009).

[19] See Frederik Balfour, "Dark Days for a Black Market: Afghanistan and Pakistan Rely Heavily on Smuggling," *Business Week*, Oct. 15, 2001.

[20] See, for example, C. Colin Davis, *The Problem of the North-West Frontier, 1890-1908* (London: Curzon Press, 1932), pp. 26-28; *Report on the Administration of the Punjab and Its Dependencies for the Year 1870-1871* (Lahore: Government Civil Secretariat Press, 1871), p. cxxxiii; *Imperial Gazetteer of India: Provincial Series, North-West Frontier Province* (Calcutta: Superintendent of Government Printing, 1908), pp. 25, 65-66.

[21] See, for example, Scott B. MacDonald, "Afghanistan," in *International Handbook on Drug Control* (Westport, CT: Greenwood Press, Scott B. MacDonald & Bruce Zagaris eds., 1992), p. 317; Linette Albert, "Afghanistan: A Perspective," in *Afghanistan in the 1970s* (New York: Praeger, Louis Dupree & Linette Albert eds., 1974), p. 257.

[22] Transnational Institute, *Downward Spiral: Banning Opium in Afghanistan and Burma*, TNI Briefing Paper Series, No. 12, June 2005.

[23] Vanda Felbab-Brown, "Asia's Role in the Illicit Trade of Wildlife," *Boston Globe*, Mar. 20, 2006.

[24] See Thomas Fuller, "Ethnic Groups in Myanmar Hope for Peace, but Gird for Fight," *New York Times*, May 11, 2009.

[25] For a history of the involvement of the junta, insurgent groups, and counterinsurgent forces in the opium trade, see Bertil Lintner, *Burma in Revolt* (Chiang Mai, Thailand: Silkworm Books, 1999).

[26] For details of the monks' peaceful protests, the junta crackdown, and subsequent political developments in Myanmar, see International Crisis Group, "Burma/Myanmar: After the Crackdown," *Asia Report No. 144*, Jan. 31, 2008.

[27] Mark McDonald, "Burmese Dissident Meets with Party," *New York Times*, Dec. 16, 2009.

[28] Nancy Lubin et al., *Narcotics Interdiction in Afghanistan and Central Asia: Challenges for International Assistance*, Report to the Open Society Institute's Central Eurasia Project and Network Women's Project, 2002.

[29] Kairat Osmonaliev, "Developing Counter-Narcotics Policy In Central Asia," Silk Road Paper, Central Asia-Caucasus Institute, Jan. 2005.

[30] Letizia Paoli et al., *The World Heroin Market: Can Supply be Cut?* (Oxford, UK: Oxford University Press, 2009), pp. 181-200.

[31] Joshua Sinai, "Islamist Terrorism and Narcotrafficking in Uzbekistan," *Defense*

and Foreign Affairs Strategic Policy, May 2000, pp. 7-8.

32 Souad Mekhennet & Michael Moss, "Europeans Get Terror Training Inside Pakistan," *New York Times,* Sept. 10, 2007.

33 *BP Statistical Review of World Energy,* June 2009, p. 6.

34 Amir Zada Asad & Robert Harris, *The Politics and Economics of Drug Production on the Pakistan-Afghanistan Border* (Burlington, VT: Ashgate, 2003); Nigel J. R. Allan, "Opium Production in Afghanistan and Pakistan," in *Dangerous Harvest: Drug Plants and the Transformation of Indigenous Landscapes* (Oxford, UK: Oxford University Press, Michael K. Steinberg et al. eds., 2004), pp. 133-52.

35 Alfred W. McCoy, *The Politics of Heroin: CIA Complicity in the Global Drug Trade* (New York: Lawrence Hill Books, revised ed. 2003), pp. 484-85; Ikramul Haq, "Pak-Afghan Drug Trade in Historical Perspective," *Asian Survey,* Oct. 1996, pp. 945-63.

36 See Lawrence Lifschultz, "Bush, Drugs and Pakistan: Inside the Kingdom of Heroin," *The Nation,* Nov. 14, 1988.

37 Ibid.

38 Asad & Harris, *The Politics and Economics of Drug Production on the Pakistan-Afghanistan Border.*

39 Author's interviews with former civilian and military officials in NWFP, fall 2008 and spring 2009.

40 Author's interviews with UNODC, Indian, and Pakistani officials, New York, Kashmir, India, and Washington, DC, spring through fall 2008.

41 Ahmed Rashid, *Taliban: Militant Islam, Oil and Fundamentalism in Central Asia* (New Haven: Yale University Press, 2001).

42 See, for example, Syed Irfan Ashraf, "Militancy and the Black Economy," *Dawn,* Mar. 22, 2009; Sabrina Taversine, "Organized Crime in Pakistan Feeds Taliban," *New York Times,* Aug. 29, 2009; Pir Zubair Shah & Jane Perlez, "Pakistan Marble Helps Taliban Stay in Business," *New York Times,* July 14, 2008.

43 General Stanley McChrystal, the top U.S. and NATO commander in Afghanistan, has indicated that he in fact intends NATO to shift to such more complex metrics. See Karen DeYoung, "U.S. Sets Metrics to Assess War Success," *Washington Post,* Aug. 30, 2009. For discussion of how such metrics should look for counternarcotics policy, see Vanda Felbab-Brown et al., "Assessment of the Implementation of the United States Government's Support for Plan Colombia's Illicit Crops Reduction Components," *USAID,* Apr. 2009.

7 | Rough Terrain: The Human Terrain System in Afghanistan

by Vanessa M. Gezari

The soldiers gathered in a makeshift conference room where fine dust coated the table and maps hung on the walls. It was March 2009 at a small U.S. Army base in Maiwand, an agricultural district in southern Afghanistan. The maps on the walls showed the area around the base in careful detail: the villages, shallow valleys and fields, the thin band of Highway 1 running west from Kandahar. Army Lt. Terrence Paul Dunn stood in front of the map, pointing to a rectangular patch of fields and compounds across a low stretch of land a few hundred yards from the base. This was Pir Zadeh, the friendliest village in his unit's operating area.

The soldiers sat on benches along the wall. They were young, with regulation haircuts and a mix of boredom and nervousness in their eyes. Among them were two civilians, members of an experimental Army project called the Human Terrain System that embeds anthropologists and other social scientists with combat units to advise soldiers about local culture.[1] One was a big man with a full beard and extra clips of ammunition strapped to his chest, while the other wore wire-rimmed glasses with his Army-issue camouflage.

Dunn traced the route they would take. Pir Zadeh lay within sight of the base, but it was too risky to walk. They would drive in MRAPs, heavily armored vehicles designed to minimize the effects of improvised bombs, then dismount and move west through the village on foot. They would work their way along a narrow alley where, if they were attacked, they could be easily boxed in.

The soldiers would create a secure perimeter as they moved, Dunn told them. Any villager who wanted to pass the patrol would have to enter the perimeter and be frisked for weapons. Watch your spacing, he told the men. Be careful when you pass intersections, where someone might see you before you see him. There would be houses all along the lane where they walked. Someone could ambush them just by opening a front door.

"Today we're maintaining lots of standoff," Dunn said. "We're going to make sure that people who are in our perimeter stay in our perimeter, and people who are outside stay outside."

The men nodded. This semi-urban topography made them anxious, though the surrounding open dunes weren't much better. Eight years into the war, Dunn and the other soldiers of the Second Battalion, Second Regiment of the First Infantry Division, known as Task Force 2-2, were the first international troops to patrol this section of southern Afghanistan in significant numbers. Most days, the sand flats and wheat and poppy fields were deceptively quiet. Complacency was easy, but its consequences could be severe. Maiwand was a key transit area for fighters and drugs, and the Taliban controlled it, intimidating people who knew the local government couldn't protect them. For a period during the past fall, more IEDs were planted there than any other place in Afghanistan or Iraq. In October 2008, insurgents pulled passengers off a bus passing through Maiwand and beheaded them, leaving the bodies near the road.

Like everything the military was doing in this new phase of its long-running war in Afghanistan, the deployment of U.S. soldiers to Maiwand was an experiment. So, too, was the Human Terrain project, and the roadmap to security and development envisioned by the bespectacled social scientist joining the patrol that day. Dr. Karl Slaikeu had asked for this patrol. A 64-year-old psychologist and conflict resolution specialist from Texas, Karl had been nursing an idea that he thought could change the course of the war.

Karl had been in Afghanistan just over a month and his previous international experience consisted of mentoring Liberian immigrants through his church. But he was confident in his understanding of human psychology. He was looking for a place where real security and development were possible—a village that, with concerted attention, could be turned into a model of stability. Pir Zadeh, where the patrol was bound, had the potential to become just such a model, Karl thought. The village was an anomaly in Maiwand, a place where locals had formed a neighborhood watch to keep intruders out and where the village elder seemed to like Americans.

Lt. Dunn wrapped up his briefing. After visiting the village elder, they would take an alternate route back to avoid a bridge they'd heard the insurgents wanted to bomb and a frequently used access road. Three potential suicide bombers were said to be roaming the area in the guise of a mullah, a woman, and a 12-year-old boy.

"All right," Dunn said. "Any questions?"

The bearded Human Terrain team member, who went by the nickname Banger, asked what to do if the patrol came under attack.

"If we take contact, you guys are getting down," Dunn said. "You're going to stay down until instructed otherwise, obviously finding cover. Anything will do, little divots in the ground. Anything's better than nothing."

Before heading out, Banger and Karl huddled with their Afghan-American interpreter. Banger was a former Marine whose background had prepared him for missions like this, but Karl had never been to a war zone. Like the other social scientists on the Human Terrain teams, he had been offered the option of carrying a weapon, and been issued an M-16. He had hunted as a boy in Nebraska and spent an afternoon practicing on a range in Texas with a buddy before deploying. But he acknowledged it wasn't enough.

Now Banger told Karl to be aware of his surroundings when interviewing villagers. If we're attacked, he told the older man, wait until the last minute to shoot.

"Only engage if you have to," Banger said. "That avoids any accidental perceptional issues, not knowing where anybody is."

"Got it," Karl said.

* * *

Karl and Banger had good reason to be watchful. On a clear day in November 2008, a Human Terrain social scientist named Paula Loyd and two of her teammates walked with a group of soldiers to a village less than half a mile from the base where Karl and Banger sat. A 36-year-old from Texas, Paula had long blonde hair and a wide, heart-shaped smile, degrees from Wellesley and Georgetown and years of experience as a soldier and aid worker in Afghanistan. On a lane near the bazaar, she interviewed Afghan villagers. She talked to a man holding a jug of gasoline, asking him about the price of fuel. Then without warning, the Afghan doused her with gas and set her on fire.

The soldiers and one of Paula's Human Terrain teammates, a 46-year-old former Army Ranger named Don Ayala, caught her attacker, pinned him to the ground and slipped plastic zipcuffs onto his wrists. Don and Paula had grown close during their training in Ft. Leavenworth and on their rocky desert base in Maiwand. When he heard that she had been badly burned, he pulled out his pistol and shot her attacker in the head.

Paula was flown to Brooke Army Medical Center in her hometown of San Antonio, where she died in January 2009. Don pleaded guilty to manslaughter in the killing of her attacker and, in May, was sentenced to five years probation. Paula was the third Human Terrain social scientist killed in the field in nine months. Dr. Karl Slaikeu had been sent to take her place.

Known to his teammates as Doc, Karl had attended seminary as a young man and considered following his Baptist minister father into the church. Instead, he got a Ph.D. in psychology, taught at the University of South Carolina, and started a conflict resolution business for corporate and private clients in Austin. In the eight years since the 9/11 attacks, as his Marine son deployed to Baghdad and he watched the U.S. slip deeper into two complex wars, Karl had grown impatient and frustrated by his own helplessness. The possibility of his son's death in combat forced him to think hard about U.S. policy.

"As a parent, I had to prepare to lose him if he was going to be over there," Karl said. "So I had to decide, 'What do I think about this?'"

He began reading everything he could find on U.S. policy in the Middle East, looking for ways that ordinary citizens like him could engage and sacrifice. Then he heard about a new Army project called the Human Terrain System. Born of a realization within the Pentagon that soldiers and commanders don't have enough cultural knowledge to win irregular wars in Iraq and Afghanistan, the project embeds civilian social scientists with combat units to advise soldiers about a range of factors that might be influencing the civilian population, from economics to tribal structures to local politics. The first Human Terrain team deployed in 2007, and today there are roughly 15 teams in Iraq. In January 2009, U.S. Central Command asked the project to more than double the number of teams it deploys to Afghanistan, from six to 13. With another 30,000 U.S. troops on the way in 2010, the number of Human Terrain teams in Afghanistan is projected to double yet again over the next 12 to 18 months.

The project is emblematic of a bigger change sweeping the Army under the leadership of General David Petraeus, the architect of the Iraq "surge" and co-author of the U.S. Army/Marine Corps Counterinsurgency Field Manual. Unlike the "shock and awe" tactics used during the invasion of Iraq, counterinsurgency is low-tech and intuitive, focused on understanding and meeting the needs of local communities to win them away from the enemy. Soldiers in Maiwand spend more time offering to dig wells than shooting Taliban, and yet they are still trained primarily to fight and kill. They lack a nuanced understanding of their environment or the skills needed to obtain one, and in a counterinsurgency, that's a fatal shortfall.

"You can't establish a democracy, build a school, build a banking system unless you know something about the society that you're working in," said Montgomery McFate, an anthropologist with a Ph.D. from Yale who runs the project with retired Special Forces Col. Steve Fondacaro.

Military commanders and the project's architects say that it helps make soldiers more knowledgeable and minimizes casualties and civilian deaths. But even before the first Human Terrain teams deployed, two things became clear: The number of highly trained academics and other social scientists with extensive knowledge or experience in Afghanistan and Iraq is extremely limited, and most of them don't want anything to do with the military.

In 2007, the American Anthropological Association came out against the project on the grounds that anthropologists working alongside soldiers would become indistinguishable from the military, making it hard for Human Terrain team members to clearly identify themselves to civilians and impossible for their subjects to freely consent to be interviewed. The anthropological association also noted that the information gathered by the Human Terrain teams could be used to target opponents in combat, violating ethics rules requiring that subjects not be harmed in the course of research. Despite contractor pay in 2007 and 2008 of $250,000 and higher for a course of training and a six-month tour, few scholars wanted to join; some feared being blacklisted in academia if they took part. (In early 2009, Human Terrain team members became government employees, a change that cut their pay by roughly a third.)

When Karl first learned of the Human Terrain project, he wasn't sure they would want someone like him, a conflict resolution specialist who had never been to Afghanistan. He also wasn't sure he wanted to join an effort that had been so intensely criticized. He studied and prayed over the ethical questions that might come up if he took the job. He wrote in his journal and talked it over with friends, academics, and his wife. He eventually decided to join, but he still harbored misgivings. As he went through the four-month training at Ft. Leavenworth, he constantly re-evaluated the project, he said. He was still doing that in Maiwand, watching for lapses, anything that might endanger local people.

"It just hasn't come," he said, speaking of a potential ethical conflict, "and I've been looking for it."

Most days, Karl worked with Banger. His real name was Stephen James Lang, but everyone called him by his nickname, which he'd earned playing rugby. He was 40, weighed nearly 300 pounds in his body armor and scowled through his thick beard. But he could talk to almost anyone and wore a beaded bracelet beneath the cuff of his camouflage uniform, a gift from his teenage daughter.

Banger had grown up on a farm near Sioux City, Iowa and served in the Marines for 11 years before injuries forced him out. He moved home to Arizona and went back to school, studying political science and taking courses on Islam. He had served in Iraq during the first Gulf War and later in Saudi Arabia, but like Karl, he had never been to Afghanistan.

In Maiwand, Banger used his childhood experiences on the farm, where he walked the beans in the morning before heading off to school, to connect with the farmers he met on patrol. But his most important job was to protect Karl, who, at 6-foot-3 with a shock of sparkling white hair, made an easy target.

* * *

On the morning of the patrol to Pir Zadeh, Karl and Banger piled into MRAPs with Dunn and his soldiers. In Banger's vehicle, "Waiting" by the metal band Trapt blared from the speakers:

I've been waiting for you
To capture my imagination
Cause I've been fooled by the illusions in my head

The convoy pulled onto Highway 1, passing a billboard with a picture of a little girl reaching for a bomb in a roadside ditch while an old man pulls her away. "To the older people: It's your responsibility to save your children from IEDs," the sign read.

They rolled past the bazaar, rows of rickety wooden stalls lining the road. A suicide bombing there in January had launched Karl on his current mission. The soldiers with whom he was now riding had been patrolling the bazaar when a man strapped with explosives blew up in front of them. Two U.S. soldiers and an Afghan interpreter were killed, along with 15 civilians; 53 Americans and Afghans were hurt.

That winter, Karl and Banger had been at an Army training center in Louisiana when Karl heard about the bombing. "How the hell did that happen?" Karl thought, and then answered his own question: "They're walking through a village that's not secure and they get blown up."

That started him thinking: What if soldiers provided real, dependable security to even one Afghan village? If the village were actually safe—something that couldn't be said of any community in Maiwand—development and jobs could follow. Afghans would see what progress looked like, instead of just hearing about it. Soldiers could hold it up as an example.

In counterinsurgency theory, this is called the "oil spot" strategy. It was devised by the French soldier and administrator Louis Hubert Lyautey, who was sent to govern colonial Morocco and Indochina in the late 19th and early 20th centuries. In Hanoi, he watched as soldiers set up a network of military posts to protect villagers and keep out insurgents, and armed locals to defend themselves. With security came "roads, telegraphs, markets ... so that with pacification, a great band of civilization advances like a spot of oil," Lyautey wrote.[2]

In the months before his deployment, Karl's enthusiasm for this approach had grown so deep, sustained and noticeable that Banger and others had taken to calling him Oil Spot Spock. He envisioned soldiers securing a single village or area—the first drop of oil—and using its success to spread safety and development drop by drop. Villagers in places like Pir Zadeh, where the patrol was headed that day, could self-select for the strategy based on their willingness to side with coalition forces against the Taliban. Meanwhile, areas outside the chosen villages would be treated as battle zones, and soldiers patrolling them would know unequivocally that they were at war. If the conflict were divided into hot and cool zones, Karl thought, soldiers could focus their humanitarian aid and development efforts in friendly areas and fight in unfriendly ones. They might have a better chance of avoiding an explosion like the one in the bazaar.

The convoy pulled off the paved road onto sand flats, lurching over dunes and finally rolling to a halt at the edge of a dense, green wheat field. The soldiers saw a man walking with a little girl and asked him to lift his shirt to make sure there wasn't a bomb strapped to his chest. Banger watched disapprovingly. Asking villagers to lift their clothes was disrespectful, and might earn the Americans more enemies than friends. There must be a less obtrusive way to search people, he thought.

But the soldiers of 1st Platoon didn't take chances. Since the bombing in the bazaar, they patrolled tensely, calling in air support whenever helicopters were nearby, searching villagers thoroughly even when they seemed friendly, and patrolling with their guns up and at the ready. Lt. Dunn, a 24-year-old high school basketball player with a degree in political science from Virginia Tech, had taken over after the bombing tore a chunk out of the previous platoon leader's arm. He knew that helicopters buzzing overhead frightened the locals they were trying to win over, but their presence also intimidated the insurgents.

The patrol wound its way through a web of alleys surrounded on both sides by high walls of yellow mud. Arched doorways led to smooth mud passageways, mysterious and medieval. A stream of clear water flowed alongside the lane, which was shaded by mulberry and pomegranate trees. Banger struck up a conversation with a group of kids. There was no school in the village, they told him, and no teachers.

After a half hour's walk, the patrol rounded a corner and came to the gate of the village elder's compound. The elder had a white beard and white turban, sun-baked skin and leathery hands covered in dirt. He smiled at Dunn, revealing a few missing teeth. When Dunn asked about security, the old man was grave. A Taliban emissary had been coming to the village to threaten him and ask for wheat seeds, he said. The Americans had given out free seeds in an attempt to cut poppy cultivation, and now the Taliban wanted them.

"Why do they want wheat seeds?" Dunn asked.

They want them to eat, the old man said, to grind into flour.

"Tell them you don't have any more," Dunn said. "You can't give them what you don't have."

Dunn pulled a business card from the pocket of his uniform. On it was printed an emergency phone number for the American base.

"Just remember that if the Taliban come in your village, or any bad guys, just give us a call," he said.

The old man took the card reluctantly. He didn't have a phone, he told the lieutenant. And everyone knew that the phones didn't work at night, when the Taliban made their rounds, because the insurgents coerced local cell phone operators to shut down their towers.

Karl had been listening to the conversation, writing quickly in his small field notebook. He sensed the old man's frustration. There weren't enough

U.S. and Afghan soldiers in Maiwand to provide reliable security, and the Afghan police didn't leave their barracks at night. But if the troops focused their limited resources on securing Pir Zadeh, perhaps by patrolling there day and night, they might have a decent chance of winning the elder's loyalty.

The Americans reached for the old man's hand. He clasped their hands in his. Everyone smiled and said goodbye, and the Americans walked off toward the spot where their armored vehicles were parked. Banger and Karl went with them.

* * *

Over the spring and summer, Karl sketched a blueprint for the oil spot strategy in Maiwand. He called his approach "Oil Spot Plus" because it was based on a tradeoff in which villagers would cooperate with international forces on security in return for services like water, electricity, health care and education. He envisioned negotiated agreements between villagers and international soldiers. The model could work in a village like Pir Zadeh, but after talking with Afghans and others on his team, Karl shifted his focus to other villages near the bazaar, where municipal government offices could act as an anchor. He hoped that more settlements would be inspired to follow. "Each oil spot is a visible manifestation of the desired end state for the entire war," Karl wrote in a paper published in the spring of 2009 in *Small Wars Journal*, an online magazine focused on counterinsurgency.[3]

With his background in conflict resolution, Karl saw the relationship between Afghans and international forces as akin to a troubled marriage, in which each side's entrenched views had to be revised if they were to get along amicably. But the reality in Afghanistan was infinitely messier. There was no baseline trust between Afghans and coalition forces on which to build the deals he hoped for, especially in Maiwand. And even if soldiers did strike a deal with the people they thought were stakeholders, that didn't mean the Afghans would be powerful enough to enforce it, or that they wouldn't strike a contradictory deal with insurgents or local warlords who didn't share the coalition's interests. Still, Karl knew that the current approach wasn't working. "The days of throwing money at the problem by digging a well, building a school or opening a clinic—without first establishing a secure perimeter in cooperation with villagers—should end," he wrote. "The old model is too risky, since an IED or other attack can turn the effort into naught in an instant."

In the selected Oil Spot villages, he suggested buying and burning the current poppy harvest and immediately transitioning to a different crop. He also wanted to start a paid informant program, quickly creating income for unemployed villagers who might otherwise work with the Taliban. Jobs were scarce in Maiwand and a man could earn easy money by placing a mine in the road, even if he didn't support the insurgents. The local Afghan police commander suggested paying people who tipped off the security forces about the location of bombs. The strategy was ambitious: Karl's budget estimate for the first year alone was $4.5 million, not counting the informant and poppy replacement programs.

One spring day, Banger went to Kandahar to meet with a Canadian officer. He placed an excited call to Karl: the Canadians were already working on a similar initiative. They wanted to know more about Karl's Oil Spot approach.

In late June, the Canadians unveiled their own "model village" initiative in Dand district, south of Kandahar. In the village of Deh-e-Bagh, they established security, erected solar-powered streetlights and put 120 villagers to work on irrigation improvements and other projects. General Stanley McChrystal, the new U.S. commander in Afghanistan, flew down to visit the village, strolling around with Canadian Brigadier General Jonathan Vance. He called the initiative "valuable," and said he wanted to see similar efforts around Afghanistan. Karl pushed excitedly forward with his own project.

Then, in mid-July, the Taliban attacked Deh-e-Bagh, killing one Afghan policeman and wounding seven others. "Because it's such a threat to the insurgency, it makes it a likely target," Canadian Major Mario Couture told the Canadian Press news agency. "Is this a surprise? No. Are they going to try again? Most likely. But the place is well-defended."[4]

Karl was still optimistic. But in Maiwand, too, violence was rising.

In late July 2009, Karl was at breakfast in the dining tent on the American base in Maiwand where he lived. He had just taken a bite out of a bagel with strawberry cream cheese when a 107 mm mortar landed with a colossal boom about 50 meters away. He hit the floor, then ran for a nearby bunker.

The following day, he and Banger accompanied a patrol to a village nearby. Banger had been there before, but the mood had chilled. "Something's different here," Banger told Karl. "It wasn't like this before."

They climbed into their armored vehicles and headed back toward the base. Five minutes later, the ground ahead of them exploded. A giant plume of black smoke rose, and the MRAP carrying Banger and Karl ground to a halt. "Oh shit," someone said. The vehicle in front of them had hit an IED.

It took hours for a recovery crew to arrive, search the area for more bombs and load the disabled MRAP onto a truck. Medics treated the soldiers, none of whom was seriously hurt. Karl and Banger sat inside the air-conditioned hull of their heavy vehicle, munching handfuls of Swedish Fish that one soldier's wife had mailed over.

Karl thought about Michael Bhatia, a Human Terrain social scientist who had died in eastern Afghanistan when his Humvee drove over an IED in May 2008. He thought about Paula Loyd, who had emailed her mother before she was attacked to tell her not to worry because "we are riding around in these new vehicles that look like tanks and I have lots of security around all the time."[5]

"Of course, it doesn't protect you in the situation she was in," Karl said later.

When the disabled MRAP had been hauled away, Banger and Karl's vehicle roared to life again. The convoy slowly rolled back, stopping at one of the smaller bases on the way to the big one.

At the chow hall, Banger grabbed bottles of cold water and loaded trays with quesadillas while Karl waited in the gravel lot. He stared at the three MRAPs parked in a line. There had been four when they left with that morning. Later, he would joke that everyone had better stay away from him. He'd endured two near misses in two days. He couldn't say what would happen next.

* * *

Karl "Doc" Slaikeu typifies social scientists deployed on Human Terrain teams in Iraq and Afghanistan in only one way: he does not think like a soldier. The Human Terrain project began with the stated goal of sending anthropologists into combat zones, but today there are at least as many psychologists, sociologists and political scientists as anthropologists in the project. The lack of strict oversight for deployed teams means that they can and do perform a broad range of functions in the field, some very useful to the units they serve, others much less so. Human Terrain teams in Afghanistan have researched, with varying degrees of success, the pine nut trade, key characteristics of insurgent night letters, and the cultural context of male homosexuality. In the best cases, what unites the teams is their ability to bring to the battlefield a measure of expertise as well as what military leaders and their corporate cousins call "out-of-the-box thinking." Intuition and the maturity gained from life experience are important tools for the counterinsurgent, yet they are qualities the average young soldier lacks. And it is the youngest soldiers—18- to 20-year-old privates led by a lieutenant of about 23—who most frequently engage Afghans.

The Human Terrain project has experienced more than its share of management and organizational problems in its short life. Its social science personnel at times find themselves navigating murky ethical territory, and they are not helped by confusion within the project and the military about what constitutes intelligence in a counterinsurgency. While acknowledging that the Human Terrain project is imperfect, most Army commanders say they would rather have the teams than not. This is because the Army in particular, the biggest and most conventional of the services, has been slow to incorporate the small-scale, human-centric approaches suited to counterinsurgency. The training cycle has not kept up with the pace of deployments these last eight years. Soldiers are taught how to attack or respond to an ambush, but in Iraq and Afghanistan now, a soldier's most important task is to forge relationships with local leaders and win them away from the insurgents. Infantrymen in their teens and twenties have become *de facto* ambassadors, trying to drive a wedge between civilians and an enemy that blends easily into the landscape. While some figure out how to do this instinctively, many others need all the help they can get.

The Human Terrain System represents an ambitious and conceptually radical approach to a pressing military problem. Its birth and evolution comes at a moment when unconventional tactics, particularly those keyed to cultural knowledge, are gaining currency at the highest levels of the military. The degree to which cultural knowledge has become a focus of military effort in the last few years itself represents a profound shift from the Powell Doctrine's emphasis on overwhelming force, powerful munitions and technology. For the Army, talking seriously about the need for cultural knowledge and understanding the population would have been tantamount to heresy when the war in Afghanistan began in 2001.

The Human Terrain System is only the first and best-known program seeking to fill this culture gap. In the Pentagon, where "culture" has become the buzzword of the moment, dozens of concepts for similar programs are bubbling up. Other services, particularly the Marines, have been working to address this shortfall in quiet, creative ways for some time. Among members of the international military community, mapping the "human terrain" has become the concept du jour in counterinsurgency operations; the Human Terrain System is a project that British, Swedish and other international forces are seeking to emulate.

Because so many people are now working on this problem, the fate of the Human Terrain project should be separated from that of the approach it embodies. By embedding social scientists, and particularly anthropologists, with combat units, the project stepped into the center of a philosophical debate over the role of the academy and social science disciplines in military and intelligence operations that has been contentious in this country since the Vietnam War. The notion of using some kind of cultural knowledge or population-centric intelligence to win 21st century wars, however, is less controversial. More time will be needed to gauge the overall success of the Human Terrain project. Meanwhile, a growing number of anthropologists and social scientists are working in various capacities to make the military smarter about the people it is fighting among, and the military is finally listening.

ENDNOTES

1 For more information on the Human Terrain System, see http://humanterrainsystem.army.mil. See also Jacob Kipp et al., "The Human Terrain System: A CORDS for the 21st Century," *Military Review*, Sept./Oct. 2006; Steve Featherstone, "Human Quicksand for the U.S. Army, a Crash Course in Cultural Studies," *Harper's Magazine*, Sept. 2008; George Packer, "Knowing the Enemy: Can Social Scientists Redefine the 'War on Terror'?" *New Yorker*, Dec. 2008. For a critical view from a military perspective, see Maj. Ben Connable, "All Our Eggs in a Broken Basket," *Military Review*, Mar./Apr. 2009. For a critical view from an academic perspective, see Roberto J. González, *American Counterinsurgency: Human Science and the Human Terrain* (Chicago: Prickly Paradigm Press, 2009).

2 Quoted in William A. Hoisington, Jr., *Lyautey and the French Conquest of Morocco* (New York: St. Martin's Press, 1995), p. 7.

3 "Winning the War in Afghanistan: An Oil Spot Plus Strategy for Coalition Forces," Karl A. Slaikeu, *Small Wars Journal*, Apr. 20, 2009.

4 Dene Moore, "Taliban Target Canadian Model Village Project in Kandahar Province," *Canadian Press*, July 14, 2009.

5 Quoted in Pamela Constable, "A Terrain's Tragic Shift," *Washington Post*, Feb. 18, 2009; later confirmed in my own correspondence with Patty Ward, Paula's mother.

8 The Enemy: Understanding and Defeating Jihadist Ideology

by Sebastian Gorka

Twenty years after the collapse of the Soviet Union and more than eight years after the 9/11 attacks, the West is still groping for strategic and doctrinal clarity. From its very beginnings in 1947-1949, the basic nature of the Cold War was understood by those who needed to understand it. The doctrinal and strategic issues were settled early on by the likes of George Kennan, Harry Truman, and George Marshall. Their prescriptions for fighting the Cold War, set by 1949, remained fundamentally unchanged for forty years and eventually brought victory. This fact is all too easy to forget.

Not only did the West win that ideological conflict, but it did so in the way that Sun Tzu described as the ultimate form of conquest: victory without fighting.[1] Unfortunately, the lack of a conventional form of victory, such as that at the end of World War II—and all that such a victory entails—allowed us to muddle through the following decade with a distinct lack of understanding of what the post-Cold War world held in store. What were armies for after the collapse of the USSR and Warsaw Pact? Yes, numerous theories were crafted to help explain the post-Cold War world, from Francis Fuku-yama's *The End of History and the Last Man* to Samuel Huntington's *The Clash of Civilizations and the Remaking of World Order*. But none of these addressed the fundamental question of what national security now meant, and what armies were for in an age of "post-industrial" war.[2]

The challenges were numerous: from how to respond to ethnic cleansing in Europe's backyard to the explosion of organized crime and the proliferation of weapons of mass destruction. Yet nothing was done, in any radical sense, to reassess the nature of the threat environment and match capabilities to challenges. In fact, the first Gulf War simply reinforced core aspects of industrial war and our belief in large-scale fire and maneuver warfare. After ten years of this malaise and "lurching for the snooze button," September 11, 2001 arrived.

Almost immediately after 9/11, members of the Bush White House and the coterie of so-called neoconservative thinkers in and around Washington declared that the geopolitics of the new century were now clear. To quote Charles Krauthammer, al-Qaeda and similar forms of Islamist terror posed a new "existential threat" to America and the West.[3] America subsequently declared a "Global War on Terrorism," and initiated regime changes in Afghanistan and Iraq.

Yet not everyone agreed with this core assessment. There are those who argue that while al-Qaeda is a murderous and deadly organization, it does not pose an overarching threat to the community of democratic Western nations.[4] To these people, two points must be made. Not only is al-Qaeda the most powerful terrorist group of the modern age, killing thousands in a matter of minutes, but it achieved something the Soviet Union never did: the mass murder of Americans (and other nationals) on U.S. soil—and later in Spain, the U.K., and elsewhere. While this mutation of the anti-Soviet mujahidin movement of the 1980s does not possess regiments of T-80 tanks or batteries of SS-20 missiles, it is more disturbing than the U.S.S.R. was in one key respect. For although Khrushchev may have rhetorically promised to "bury us," he and his Kremlin successors never took the step of initiating conflict against America and its allies, since he and his administration were fundamentally rational actors constrained and deterred by the thought of nuclear retaliation. Osama bin Laden is wholly different. He has declared repeatedly that he intends to use weapons of mass destruction as soon as he can acquire them. Against his ilk deterrence policy has no effect.

My chapter concludes this volume by discussing how the United States failed to adequately identify the nature of the conflict it embarked upon in response to the 9/11 attacks, our flawed understanding of the enemy, and the fact that today we are just beginning to appreciate the central role of religious ideology in this war. Should we continue to misunderstand these three realities of the post-9/11 world, success in Afghanistan and Pakistan will not be achievable.

THE AFTERMATH OF SEPTEMBER 11

Given how horrific the attacks against Washington, New York, and Flight 93 were, it is reasonable to state that America's post-9/11 sphere of mobility was truly enormous. There are few theoretical response scenarios that would have been out of the question, given the sentiments felt around the world as televised images of the attacks were broadcast globally again and again. And as the nation's political elite declared the threat to be existential, it was reasonable to expect a large-scale response.

Given that three-quarters of the 9/11 hijackers came from Saudi Arabia, as did bin Laden, and that some of the highest members of the Saudi government had been known to fund al-Qaeda, logically a response targeting Saudi Arabia in some way would have been justified. In addition to Saudi Arabia, there was (and is) another obvious candidate. If there is one nation in the world that has undoubtedly sponsored international terrorism over the last thirty years, from the Middle East to the Balkans, it is Iran. Even a most restrictive interpretation of national security should have made the targeting of Iran an obvious choice.[5]

Indeed, instead of addressing these two threats, the Bush administration chose to move first against al-Qaeda's headquarters in Afghanistan. This was also justified, especially in terms of disrupting the organization's operational capabilities and neutralizing key figures—and the operation was very successful in doing just that. But to posit that a lasting blow would be struck against Salafist terrorism without cutting off the financial, logistical and ideological support of Saudi Arabia was, to say the least, wrongheaded. Instead, the choice was made to invade Iraq and effect regime-change there.

With respect to the invasion of Iraq, one point must be made clear. Whatever one's political leaning, and whatever one's attitude toward international affairs, it is incontestable that Saddam Hussein ranks with Joseph Stalin and Pol Pot as one of the most heinous and murderous leaders in all of history. He was, and remains, the only leader in history to have used weapons of mass destruction against his own people. He was responsible for the slaughter of Kurds, Iranians and Kuwaitis, and for the torture and death of hundreds of thousands of Iraqis.

Despite this, the case for war against Iraq was badly argued by the administration and badly prepared—or, rather, the post-war game plan was badly prepared. On the question of how the war was justified, the need to locate

Saddam Hussein's weapons of mass destruction should have been understood as irrelevant. The facts are incontrovertible: at the end of the Gulf War, Saddam Hussein admitted to coalition forces and the United Nations that he had manufactured and stockpiled literally tons of chemical weapons. In refusing to provide proof of their destruction, he was technically in breach of ceasefire for the period between 1991 and 2003. As a result, the use of force was legal by the standards of international law.[6]

The details of the invasion are well known, and are being evermore precisely detailed.[7] The question for us is, what are the consequences of the invasion and the situation that followed? From the operational point of view, the situation is not that dark, since once again we have witnessed the immeasurable ability of the U.S. fighting man to adapt to new and challenging conditions. The problem is less one of operational flexibility and adaptability than one of perceptions: of the United States having lost its pole position.

During the Cold War, America truly did represent the values that were behind its foreign policy rhetoric. It did not have to convince the oppressed peoples of the Communist bloc of the veracity of the American dream. But today there is convincing to be done: as Joshua T. White's chapter makes clear, one factor that significantly aided the Muttahida Majlis-e-Amal's (MMA) electoral rise in 2002 was the U.S. invasion of Afghanistan. This convincing has to be undertaken in a completely different cultural milieu. This is why the old tools of strategic communication must be reassessed. The various plans for alternative Arab radio and TV channels do not take into account the fact that Radio Free Europe and Radio Liberty were broadcast to members of the same cultural and civilizational group as ourselves.

GLOBAL INSURGENCY OR NOT?

As we await the Obama administration's new National Security Strategy, discussion in Washington revolves around the question of whether or not the conflict we are currently in is to be understood as a global insurgency, and how much prior lessons of counterinsurgency can help us to fight al-Qaeda. I would like to echo on this point the significant work done by David Kilcullen, formerly of the State Department's Office of the Coordinator for Counterterrorism and adviser to General Petraeus.[8] To paraphrase Kilcullen, what we are doing today is not exactly counterinsurgency but counterinsurgency is the closest model we have to the situation we face. As a result, the principles of counterinsurgency are most useful. Nevertheless, we have to understand that we are not limited strictly to a counterinsurgency scenario, since al-Qaeda is not interested in changing the political reality in just one country—for example, as the Muslim Brotherhood originally was in Egypt.[9]

Additionally, it is not simply a question of insurgency and classic counter-insurgency, since it is not a fight for national legitimacy as is always the case with such conflicts. The United States has already lost the fight of perceptions in this regard thanks to the almost universally immature political environments in the Middle East, Central Asia, and elsewhere, and thanks also to the thriving influence of conspiracy theories in countries where democracy is weak. We are not responsible for the individuals in these countries in the same way previous counterinsurgent governments have been responsible for the people that suffer from the violence of insurgency on their own territory. As a result, legitimacy in the narrow nation-state related political sense is not the goal today as it was in prior counterinsurgency campaigns that Western nations were involved with in past decades.[10]

At the same time, if we look to the official definition of what an insurgency is, we see that in most cases it is said to involve an "organized movement."[11] It is not possible to devote adequate space in this chapter to a discussion of what exactly al-Qaeda is,[12] but it is important in relationship to the question of counter-strategies to know what al-Qaeda is not.

Al-Qaeda is no longer a unitary organization. It is not—despite what the media would have us believe—a global network, at least not in the sense of a network through which bin Laden is capable of exercising command and control as he did prior to U.S. operations in Afghanistan. We must be wary of using words that carry with them intellectual "baggage" that can influence threat assessments in subjective ways. When those used to functioning in a Westphalian, state-driven milieu use the word "network," it connotes some element of master control. The network of Nazi agents uncovered and turned as a whole by British intelligence during WWII is a perfect example. This "network" was recruited, trained and deployed by Hitler's intelligence apparatus in Berlin. Then, thanks to British codebreakers, it was broken and turned to serve the unified purposes of London. Subsequently, when we use the word network for al-Qaeda and its affiliates, we at least infer that bin Laden or Zawahiri train, recruit and task groups as diverse as al-Shabaab and Abu Sayyaf. Such an inference is not substantiated by reality, especially after 2001.

Nor is al-Qaeda an ideology in the sense that we are used to, since it is largely informed by religion; faith is not something we typically associate with ideology. And lastly, it is misleading to portray al-Qaeda as some sort of franchise organization akin to a McDonald's—which, no matter where you are, provides you with the same Big Mac.[13] To truly be such a franchise it would need a functioning headquarters, a universally accepted end-state for all its members, and each unit would have to have exactly the same skill-sets.

Al-Qaeda proper is today a remnant of its former self. It has connected to several groups around the world, groups which self-associate with the image and rhetoric of al-Qaeda but often seek to achieve some local and far more limited goal. This heterogeneous aspect of what we today misleadingly term al-Qaeda is important. Let me illustrate this with one brief anecdote. During a Defense Department-sponsored course on counterterrorism, it was pointed out to me by a colonel from Pakistani military intelligence that the most popular boy's name in his country in the past twelve months was Osama. I responded to this astonishing fact by asking whether this means bin Laden enjoys the popular support of most Pakistanis. Of course not, the colonel replied: there is hardly anyone in his country who would wish to live in a "caliphate" under the leadership of Osama bin Laden. Yet while the strategic aims bin Laden espouses and the tools he uses are anathema to most Pakistanis, many Pakistanis sympathize when he refers to issues such as the freedom of Palestine or the sanctity of Mecca and Medina. It is this kind of cognitive dissonance that makes our understanding of al-Qaeda so difficult, and which differentiates it from unified and centralized ideologies of the past, such as Nazism, Fascism, and Communism.

What then is the model that will help us to understand and defeat al-Qaeda? I agree with the writings of Fred Kagan of the American Enterprise Institute, who advises us to compare the al Qaeda of today with the Bolsheviks of the early 1900s prior to the Russian Revolution of 1917.[14] I think the analogy is a useful one, given that we can reasonably portray Communism as a secular religion instigated by a tiny minority, without the support of the millions of people on whose behalf the Bolsheviks claimed to act. But instead of comparing al-Qaeda with the pre-Revolutionary Bolsheviks, I see it as more informative to understand our enemy as the equivalent of that "vanguard" group of extremists at a point after 1917, after a *failed* revolution—to see al-Qaeda as totalitarian merchants of political violence who are now in hiding, who enjoy the permissive yet uninformed support of many more, and whose significance or apparent size seems to increase as more and more local actors and groups self-associate with their ideas or beliefs.

Unfortunately, the similarities between this ideological conflict and the previous one that shaped world affairs for most of the twentieth century have been oversimplified, or missed entirely. The debate about how to provide for America's security in a post-Cold War and post-9/11 world has stubbornly remained quite superficial.

COIN VERSUS CT

Since President Obama took office there has at the highest levels developed a debate concerning Afghanistan, as to whether our focus should be counter-insurgency (COIN), which is favored by Gen. Stanley McChrystal's camp, or counterterrorism (CT), which is favored by Vice President Joe Biden's camp. Daveed Gartenstein-Ross has outlined the contours of this debate, and the process by which the administration ultimately embraced COIN in Afghanistan, in the introduction to this volume.

While it is true that an insurgent can use terrorist tactics, the differences between the two types of actors are significant. Insurgency has as its goal changing the whole regime which it targets, and has the capacity to do so thanks to mass mobilization. Terrorism, in contrast, is a weapon of weaker or more marginal groups, and usually tries to force an alteration in just one element of a regime, in just perhaps one policy (the Provisional IRA, for example, which sought autonomy for Northern Ireland). In other words, insurgencies wish to (and often can) become the government, while terrorists more often wish to affect the behavior of governments because they do not have the ability to build a "counter-state."[15]

Al-Qaeda and Associated Movements (AQAM) fit neither category easily. Bin Laden has with his violence targeted specific policies of numerous governments, from the U.S.'s deployment on the Arabian peninsula to Spain's troop deployments in Iraq. But AQAM also wishes to encourage the use of force to remove "apostate" heads of Arab regimes, and its declared goal is to create a caliphate. Thus, positioning the enemy as either an insurgent or a terrorist seems simplistic. Whether we are looking at the Taliban in Afghanistan, Abu Sayyaf in the Philippines, or al-Shabaab in Somalia, these groups are inextricably linked to a broader narrative that melds classic political terrorism with ideas of theocratic domination.

Since terrorism and insurgency are both forms of unconventional conflict, it may be worthwhile at this point to refer to the work of master strategist Colin Gray and his understanding of irregular warfare.[16] For Gray, warfare is the same in its fundamental aspects whatever its outward guise, whether the conflict is counterinsurgency or inter-bloc thermonuclear war. Both are forms of war. Subsequently it is important to remind ourselves of Carl von Clausewitz's warning: war is simple, but it is not easy.[17] This holds for inter-state war just as much for counterinsurgency or counterterrorism. Additionally, we should remind ourselves that knowledge does not equal operational success. One may have read all the works from Sun Tzu to Clausewitz and T.E. Lawrence and beyond, and internalized all the truths they contain, but this in no way guarantees the skill or ability to implement that knowledge. The gulf between theory and practice in warfare is huge because it is not a hard science, and because it concerns the activities, wills, and intentions of human beings—not machines or ineluctable forces of nature.

It has been pointed out that in past counterinsurgency campaigns, after the application of brute military force came the period of winning hearts and minds (WHAM). We have done very little in the past eight years on the ideational front of this war. In fact, we have often undermined ourselves by allowing political correctness and unreasonable sensitivity to religion to facilitate the enemy's domination of the strategic communications agenda. While our operational focus should include the obvious requirement of attacking both the capability and motivation of the enemy, we must understand that the latter is a product of ideology that must be neutralized by a counter-ideology.[18]

In counterinsurgency it is said that the battle is won when the government demonstrates that it is more capable of providing for the security of its citizens than the insurgent is. This cannot be our goal in this conflict. It is not our job to provide for the security of Muslims everywhere. What we can do is take the war to individual groups and terrorist leaders, and win over those potential non-Western allies who already have the ability to work in cultural areas where our expertise is minimal, who can penetrate fundamentalist networks, those governments that can in fact address issues of legitimacy and bear the responsibility for providing security for their own citizens.

SHAPING THE DISCOURSE

Additionally, we need to be realistic about what can be achieved through public diplomacy and information policies, and understand the true target audience of such campaigns. The job of our "strategic communicators" and diplomats, when addressing populations that are potentially in agreement with bin Laden or who are simply indifferent, should not in the first instance be to make America look good. It is more urgent to make Osama bin Laden and the killing of innocents look bad. In the past, especially during World War II under the OSS, we were much clearer on how important it is to effectively communicate to the world that the enemy should be understood as an outsider, as someone to be shunned by all.

The trouble today is in part a product of bin Laden's ability, in the space of a few short years, to dominate the agenda of strategic communications and public discourse. If we mention the word "caliphate" to a lay-person, the first and perhaps only individual who will come to mind is bin Laden. On the other hand, if we say the word "democracy" or "liberty," it is no longer, unfortunately, the United States, a vision of the Statue of Liberty, or a Western leader that comes to mind. But it should be.

This second association can only be achieved by making bin Laden the outlaw and by repositioning America and its allies as the representatives perhaps not of democracy—with all the cultural specificity that the term entails—but certainly representatives of concepts such as liberty. We need a valid counter-doctrine to disarm the venomous myths al-Qaeda has perpetrated.

What we need today is that small group of wise men who were prepared to suggest and implement radical ideas at the end of World War II, to arrive at a theory of victory instead of what we are reduced to today, which is a "strategy" of sequential tactics. We need to not only learn the lessons of prior insurgencies and terrorist campaigns, but to practice what we have learned from those prior campaigns: most importantly, we need to return to the basics and understand in its marrow the core principle that Clausewitz left for us. When he discussed the connection between war and politics he did not mean it to be understood as it so often is today, that war is some isolated activity which occurs when politics runs out of options. No. Clausewitz's most famous sentence—war is the continuation of politics by other means[19]—was nothing more than an illumination of the unity of both activities. While it may be trite to say that politics is war, what the General meant to emphasize is that war is politics, and as such victory will only come if we are clear about the political goal we wish to achieve: we will only achieve that goal if all the tools of politics, not just force, are deployed toward that end. The application of those tools, military or otherwise, must be informed by a clear understanding of the enemy and its recent trajectory.

AL-QAEDA AND THE TALIBAN

Sun Tzu advised us that if we wish to guarantee victory, we must know two things: who we are, and who the enemy is. In regard to the Taliban and al-Qaeda, the latter question is mudded by the scores of talking heads and self-anointed military experts who have swarmed the North American media since 9/11. Far too many bandy about the terms Taliban and al-Qaeda with abandon, never taking a moment to define what they mean or to discuss the relevant links involved.

Words matter, even—or especially—when bullets are flying. The question of who the enemy is has become all the more important since the arrival of a new U.S. administration whatever the strategy that replaces George W. Bush's Global War on Terrorism, its architects must first define the nature of the enemy and the nature of the conflict we are in.

The Taliban are not al-Qaeda and al-Qaeda is not the Taliban. Yes, the Taliban gave safe haven to Osama bin Laden and his organization after he was expelled from Sudan in 1996. Yes, members of al-Qaeda and even bin Laden's own family have intermarried within Taliban power-groups, including the so-called Quetta Shura. But the Taliban must be understood as a heterogeneous group of warlords with variegated pasts and disparate interests. Some are former members of the governing regime that was dislodged after 9/11. Some are primarily narcotraffickers, while others are tribally-defined and established masters of regions that have proved impossible to domesticate for centuries. The only meaningful way in which the collective noun "Taliban"—and this is how the word should be understood—must be used, is as a descriptor for those individuals and forces who either subscribe to the fundamentalist totalitarianism that characterized Afghanistan before October 2001, or who exploit this ideology to protect vested interests.

Al-Qaeda is even harder for Western minds to comprehend clearly and realistically. Al-Qaeda the organization was not destroyed by the military and CT actions that followed 9/11, but its command-and-control capabilities have been severely degraded. It is of course linked to the Madrid and London attacks, among others, but it is no longer capable of doing the "start to finish" of globally orchestrated synchronized multiple attacks, which was its trademark attack method.

That is the good news. But conversely, while al-Qaeda's operational capability has decreased, its ideological significance has grown. It is in this less tangible arena that the historical significance of Osama bin Laden and his organization lies, because al-Qaeda represents a successful redefinition of the concept of jihad. Building on the theological and ideological arguments of such prior Salafists as Sayyid Qutb, Hassan al-Banna (founder of the Muslim Brotherhood), and Abul A'la Maududi, bin Laden and his deputy Ayman al-Zawahiri have successfully given the concept of jihad new content. In the past, jihad was used to refer to a wide range of acts that included the inner struggle of the faithful, war against apostate leaders, and even guerrilla warfare against the forces of a godless enemy (the U.S.S.R. in Afghanistan, for instance). With events such as 9/11, Madrid, and London, al-Qaeda has managed to provide a new meaning to jihad: killing civilians.[21]

AL-QAEDA AND THE IDEOLOGICAL WAR

Assumptions about al-Qaeda have a bad tendency to turn out wrong. Too many U.S. security analysts underestimated the group before the September 11 attacks, and then, not surprisingly, perhaps overestimated it after 9/11. In recent years, inside and outside the U.S. government, there was a new reigning assumption about al-Qaeda: that the appeal of its Salafi-jihadi ideology would decline as its ability to conduct terrorist attacks was eroded by intelligence, law enforcement, and military operations. Amid what appeared to be a building backlash against bin Laden's outfit among Muslims worldwide—seen most vividly in the Sunni rebellion in Iraq and the denunciation of al-Qaeda by high-profile former Salafist ideologues such as Sayyid Imam al-Sharif, a.k.a. Dr. Fadl—the assumption that al-Qaeda was growing operationally weak and ideologically moribund seemed sound.

It now seems that this assumption was quite wrong. In a closed session of international intelligence and counterterrorism officials held in 2009, a very high-ranking U.S. intelligence officer provided a simple, counterintuitive observation. Bin Laden may now be making infrequent filmed statements instead of planning and executing attacks, but those statements and the ideology behind them have grown in importance. Consequently, the U.S. intelligence community is starting to see the ideological threat as potentially a greater danger to U.S. interests than actual al-Qaeda killers.

If true, this thesis renders moot a rather unseemly debate that continues to rage within the counterterrorism community. On one side is Marc Sageman, a forensic psychiatrist and former CIA case officer, and on the other Bruce Hoffman, a professor in the Security Studies Program at Georgetown University. These two, and their followers, came to theoretical blows in 2008 over their assessments of the state of al-Qaeda. Sageman argues that the phenomenon of "leaderless jihad," wherein individuals and groups become radicalized and commit terrorism with no al-Qaeda guidance at all, has supplanted the group itself as a threat.[22] Hoffman argues, to the contrary, that bin Laden and company still pose the gravest of threats, that the operational core of al-Qaeda retains high levels of command and control, and that leaderless jihad is but a myth.[23]

It now seems that both were mistaken. Open-source information, along with the U.S. intelligence community's recent assessment, paints a different picture: al-Qaeda is operationally degraded but ideologically ascendant, with "al-Qaeda Central" continuing to exercise a significant degree of control over the shaping and dissemination of its Salafi-jihadi message, and with the coordinated acts of violence against civilians that it does manage to carry out continuing to play an important role. Al-Qaeda does not possess the organizational strength it had eight years ago, but its ideology is not waning. On the contrary, its "propaganda by the deed" continues to inspire new recruits and terrorist attacks, particularly outside the Arab world.

Recent nongovernmental data support this view of al-Qaeda. Salafi terrorism of the sort that al-Qaeda inspires and directs has reared its head in places such as the Philippines, Russia, Somalia, and Pakistan. According to figures reported by The American Security Project, the annual number of Islamist terror attacks tripled between 2004 and 2008, to nearly 600 incidents.[24] Indeed, if attacks in Afghanistan, Iraq, and Israel are removed from the total, the trend over the same four-year period is even more startling, showing a quadrupling of Salafi-inspired attacks.[25] And if you go back even further—back before 9/11, the Bush presidency, and the wars in Afghanistan and Iraq—the picture is shocking: a tenfold increase in annual terrorist attacks over the past decade.[26]

It also appears that al-Qaeda's ideology is winning converts even among Muslims who do not become foot-soldiers in the extremist cause. It may seem absurd to someone sitting in Washington when bin Laden says the West is "at war with Islam," but in Pakistan, Egypt, and elsewhere in the Muslim world a disturbingly large percentage of the population believes this is what drives U.S. counterterrorism operations. As one Pakistani officer told this author during a visit to the Middle East in the summer of 2009: "We've had enough of all the Americans in Pakistan." Joshua White's early chapter certainly helps to illuminate just this very fact.

The huge increase in terrorist violence, and the broader sympathy for al-Qaeda's aims, has occurred under the terrorist group's unique ideological banner. In the attacks that brought pandemonium to Mumbai in November 2008, though the terrorists also went after Hindus, it is clear by their active search for U.S. and British citizens and their targeting of a Jewish community center that the terrorists were dutifully following the call to jihad against the Jews and Crusaders as declared by Osama bin Laden in 1996. But this obvious ideological connection is less interesting than the ways in which the religious ideology of the Salafi jihad has influenced other parts of the world where Islamist violence was previously unknown. The best example is Chechnya—and to a lesser extent its neighboring Dagestan.

The Islam of the Caucasus was always heavily influenced by a brand of Sufism that arrived in the region only in the 18th century, and which would be tempered by totalitarianism.[27] Despite the 1991 Dudayev coup and Chechen leader Aslan Maskhadov's decision to embrace Islam as a state ideology, this version of Islam was never close historically to the extreme version of Wahhabi-inspired terrorism. Yet it became such for mujahidin fighters in the Caucasus, as testified by the bodies of 156 children in the Beslan massacre. What had been a distinctly political fight for independence from Russia thus fell victim to al-Qaeda's philosophy of Salafi jihad.

A similar ideological injection has occurred and is occurring in a completely different part of the world. But in this case we understand it even less despite its demonstrating the trend perfectly. Again, a Sufi-influenced culture is concerned, but this time in Africa. With a Muslim faith traditionally based upon the mysticism of the nomadic *wadad*, or holy man, the Islam of Somalia has survived many trials, including all-out regional war and the international Islamic revivalist movement of the 1960s and 1970s. However, it too has followed the Caucasus model toward a more extreme practice. The Islamic Courts Union and its offspring al-Shabaab—built and formerly led by Aden Hashi Ayro, who received military training at an al-Qaeda camp in Afghanistan—have succeeded where famine and civil war failed.[28] The recent arrests in Melbourne, Australia, of a Somali terrorist cell and al-Shabaab's declaration that it wishes to become an al-Qaeda affiliate signal that the U.S.'s involvement with Somalia is far from over. Not only will AFRICOM's forces be fighting piracy and trying to stabilize a country that really does not exist institutionally, but they will be attempting with other U.S. agencies to ensure that Somalia's diaspora does not pose an imminent threat to domestic U.S. interests.

CONCLUSION

What does all this mean for the conflict formerly known as the Global War on Terror? It means, to begin with, that the "surge" in Afghanistan will distract us from what the U.S. should really be doing to defeat al-Qaeda. American boots on the ground will do little to defeat al-Qaeda's ideology. Attempts to reach out to fence-sitters and those who can be won over are important, but speeches such as the one President Obama made in Cairo are simply not enough.

The U.S. needs to go on the ideological offensive. In the culture of Islam, the question of a leader's authenticity is paramount. Bin Laden and those who follow his worldview must be delegitimized. After the debacle that was strategic communications under the last administration, Washington must formulate a marginalization policy. A lead agency must be empowered by the White House, and it must coordinate a whole-of-government message that focuses primarily on the vast number of Muslim victims of al-Qaeda's brand of terrorism. The U.S. should focus less on concepts such as democracy, and more upon the bloody reality that results from al-Qaeda's ideology.

Additionally, the realities on the ground must be recognized for what they are: centuries-old political, social and economic truths. Afghanistan has never functioned as a modern nation-state based on one coherent national identity. Moreover, the Soviets and the British before them, despite huge resources and a complete lack of stultifying political correctness, proved entirely incapable of securing the Durand Line. Therefore, as we delegitimize al-Qaeda, the Taliban, and other terror groups through an active and sophisticated propaganda campaign, Washington and Kabul must recognize the legitimacy of the only political structures that have ever successfully exercised sovereignty in the area: the tribes.

In exchange for their *de facto* authority being recognized trilaterally by the U.S., the Afghan government, and Islamabad, the tribes must guarantee that their territory will never again be used by extremist forces to launch attacks on the U.S., Kabul, or Pakistan. This is one feasible strategy that can stabilize the region and deny it to our enemies.

ENDNOTES

1   Sun Tzu, *On the Art of War* (El Paso, TX: El Paso Norte Press, Lionel Giles trans., 2005), p. 125.

2   For an influential discussion on the difference between industrial and post-industrial war, see Rupert Smith, *The Utility of Force: The Art of War in the Modern*

World (New York: Penguin Books, 2006).

3   Charles Krauthammer, "This is Not Crime, This is War," *Washington Post*, Sept. 12, 2001.

4   For example Chris Preble of the Cato Institute or Peter Beinart writing in *Time*. See Chris Preble, "Countering Terrorism," in *The Cato Handbook for Policymakers* (Washington, DC: Cato Institute, 7th ed. 2009); Peter Beinart, "Amid the Hysteria, a Look at What al-Qaeda Can't Do," *Time*, Jan. 18, 2010. Even Fareed Zakaria has declared that the greatest threat is our overreaction to al-Qaeda. See Fareed Zakaria, "Don't Panic," *Newsweek*, Jan. 9, 2010.

5   For that reason, I disagree with Christine Fair's assertion elsewhere in this volume that the U.S. has "undermined its own legal and ideological commitments to nonproliferation and counterterrorism by funneling billions of dollars to Pakistan since 9/11 while being unable to forge even tactical alliances with Iran": if anything, the true surprise is that the United States has not done more to counter Iran's nefarious activities.

6   For background on relevant aspects of international law, see the excellent monograph by Michael N. Schmitt. Michael N. Schmitt, *Counter-Terrorism and the Use of Force in International Law*, Marshall Center Paper No. 5, Nov. 2002.

7   The most detailed of recent accounts is Michael R. Gordon & Bernard E. Trainor, *Cobra II : The Inside Story of the Invasion and Occupation of Iraq* (New York: Knopf Publishing Group, 2006).

8   See David Kilcullen, "Countering Global Insurgency," *Journal of Strategic Studies*, 2005.

9   The issue of how concepts of nation-state relate to Muslim fundamentalism and pan-Arabism is a crucial aspect in understanding the evolution and mindset of actors such as bin Laden. However, this is beyond the scope of the current paper.

10   For a full examination of problems that the concept of global counterinsurgency brings with it, see Stephen Sloan & Sebastian Gorka, "Contextualizing Counterinsurgency," *Journal of International Security Affairs*, Spring 2009.

11   See U.S. Dept. of Defense Joint Publication 102.

12   For more details, see Sebestyén Gorka, "Al Qaeda's Next Generation," *Terrorism Monitor* (Jamestown Foundation), June 29, 2004.

13   This argument is explicitly made in Richard Engel, "'Al-Qaida Franchises'—Ticking Time Bombs," *MSNBC*, June 7, 2007; see also Sharmine Narwani, "Looking Under My Bed for al Qaeda," *Huffington Post*, Jan. 27, 2010.

14   See Fred Kagan, "The New Bolsheviks: Understanding Al Qaeda," *National Security Outlook*, American Enterprise Institute, Nov. 2005.

15   Full a full discussion of how a threat group—insurgent or terrorist—evolves, and how to analyze an irregular campaign and plan an apposite response, see Thomas A. Marks, Sebastian L. v. Gorka & Robert Sharp, "Getting the Next War Right: Beyond Population-Centric Warfare," *PRISM*, National Defense University, forthcoming June 2010. For an even deeper examination of irregular warfare, and the role within it of the counter-state, see the seminal work Thomas A. Marks, *Maoist People's War in Post-Vietnam Asia* (Bangkok: White Lotus, 2007).

16   See Colin S. Gray, "Irregular Enemies and the Essence of Strategy: Can the Amer-

ican Way of War Adapt?," Strategic Studies Institute, U.S. Army War College, Carlisle, Penn., Mar. 2006.

17 Carl von Clausewitz, *On War*, book I, ch. VII.

18 For an introduction to strategic communications in the current context of global terrorism, see Sebastian Gorka & David Kilcullen "Who's Winning the Battle for Narrative: Al-Qaida Versus the United States and Its Allies," in *Influence Warfare*, (Westport: Praeger Security International, James J.F. Forest ed., 2009), pp. 229-240. For a masterful treatise on what we have done wrong in the war of ideas since 9/11, and what we should do now, see Robert R. Reilly, "Ideas Matter—Restoring the Content of Public Diplomacy," B. Kenneth Simon Center for American Studies, The Heritage Foundation, 2009.

19 Carl von Clausewitz, *On War* (Princeton, NJ: Princeton University Press, Michael Howard & Peter Paret eds., 1976); see also John E. Sheppard, Jr., "*On War*: Is Clausewitz Still Relevant?" *Parameters*, Sept. 1990, pp. 85-99; Martin van Creveld, *The Transformation of War* (New York: The Free Press, 1991), pp. 33–62.

20 Sun Tzu, *On the Art of War*, p. 125.

21 See Sebastian L. v. Gorka, "Understanding History's Seven Stages of Jihad," *CTC Sentinel*, Oct. 2009, pp. 15-17.

22 For an analytic summary of the debate, see John Picarelli, "The Future of Terrorism," *National Institute of Justice Journal*, Oct. 29, 2009.

23 Bruce Hoffman, "The Myth of Grass Roots Terrorism," *Foreign Affairs*, May/June 2008.

24 Bernard I. Finel & Christine Dehn, "Are We Winning?," *ASP Perspectives*, Spring 2009.

25 Ibid.

26 Ibid.

27 See Zeyno Baran et al., *Islamic Radicalism in Central Asia and the Caucasus* (Sweden: Central Asia-Caucasus Institute and Silk Road Studies Program, 2006).

28 For an overview of how Islamic militancy developed in Somalia, see Daveed Gartenstein-Ross, "The Strategic Challenge of Somalia's al-Shabaab," *Middle East Quarterly*, Fall 2009.

THE CONTRIBUTORS

EDITORS

DAVEED GARTENSTEIN-ROSS is the director of the Center for the Study of Terrorist Radicalization at the Foundation for Defense of Democracies. He has published four monographs, co-edited the book *From Energy Crisis to Energy Security* (FDD Press 2008), and wrote a memoir entitled *My Year Inside Radical Islam* (Tarcher/Penguin 2007). In addition to his academic research on terrorism, Gartenstein-Ross seeks to craft practical solutions to some of the field's vexing problems. His consulting work has included live hostage negotiations, work on border security issues, and story development for major media companies. He frequently leads training for the U.S. military and federal, state, and local law enforcement; in 2009 he received a Leader Development and Education for Sustained Peace Support Excellence Award from U.S. Army Central Command for this work. Gartenstein-Ross earned a M.A. in world politics from the Catholic University of America, where he is currently a Ph.D. candidate. He also earned a J.D. from the New York University School of Law.

CLIFFORD D. MAY is the president of the Foundation for Defense of Democracies. The *Daily Telegraph* (U.K.) named May one of the "100 most influential conservatives in America" in 2010. May has had a long and distinguished career in international relations, journalism, communications, and politics. A veteran news reporter, foreign correspondent, and editor (at the *New York Times* and other publications), he has covered stories in more than two dozen countries, including Pakistan, Iran, and China. He writes a weekly column that is nationally distributed by the Scripps Howard News Service. In 2009, the U.S. Department of State awarded him a "U.S. Speaker and Specialist Grant" for a series of speaking engagements and meetings (with government and religious leaders, academics and journalists) in Pakistan. He holds masters degrees from both Columbia University's School of International and Public Affairs and its School of Journalism, and holds a certificate in Russian language and literature from Leningrad University.

CONTRIBUTING AUTHORS

HASSAN ABBAS is Quaid-i-Azam Professor associated with the South Asia Institute, Columbia University, and a Senior Advisor at the Belfer Center for Science and International Affairs at the Kennedy School of Government, Harvard University. For 2009-2010, he has been named the Bernard Schwartz fellow at the Asia Society headquarters in New York. Abbas holds a MALD and Ph.D. from the Fletcher School of Law and Diplomacy at Tufts University, and earned a masters degree in political science from Government College Lahore, Punjab University, and an LLM in international law from School of Law, Nottingham University, UK. Before his distinguished academic career, Abbas served as a government official in the administrations of Prime Minister Benazir Bhutto (1994-1995) and President Pervez Musharraf (1999-2000). As a member of the Police Service of Pakistan, he served in field supervisory positions in the North-West Frontier Prince in the late 1990s. Abbas' acclaimed book *Pakistan's Drift into Extremism: Allah, the Army and America's War on Terror* (ME Sharpe 2004) remains on bestseller lists in Pakistan and India.

DR. C. CHRISTINE FAIR is an assistant professor at the Center for Peace and Security Studies (CPASS) within Georgetown University's Edmund A. Walsh School of Foreign Service. She earned a Ph.D. from the University of Chicago's Department of South Asian Languages and Civilization in 2004, and an M.A. from the Harris School of Public Policy. Prior to joining Georgetown, she served as a senior political scientist with the RAND Corporation, a political officer to the United Nations Assistance Mission to Afghanistan in Kabul, and as a senior research associate in the U.S. Institute for Peace's Center for Conflict Analysis and Prevention. She has authored, co-authored, and co-edited several books, and has written numerous peer-reviewed articles covering a range of security issues in Afghanistan, Bangladesh, India, Pakistan, and Sri Lanka. She is the Managing Editor of *India Review*.

DR. VANDA FELBAB-BROWN is an expert on international and internal conflict issues and their management, including counterinsurgency. She focuses particularly on the interaction between illicit economies and military conflict. She is a Fellow in Foreign Policy and in the 21st Century Defense Initiative at the Brookings Institution, where she focuses on South Asia, the Andean region, Mexico, and Somalia. A frequent commentator in the media, she is the author of *Shooting Up: Counterinsurgency and the War on Drugs* (Brookings Institution Press, 2009) which examines these issues in Colombia, Peru, Afghanistan, Burma, Northern Ireland, India, and Turkey. Prior to taking up her position at Brookings, she was an assistant professor at Georgetown University. Dr. Felbab-Brown is also the author of numerous policy reports and academic articles.

VANESSA M. GEZARI is writing a book about the work of the Human Terrain System and related efforts in Afghanistan. A journalist who covers national and international affairs with a focus on Afghanistan, South Asia, and the impact of conflict on its survivors, she lived in New Delhi and Kabul for nearly three years in the aftermath of the September 11 attacks, reporting for the *Chicago Tribune* from 2002-03 and training Afghan journalists with the Institute for War and Peace Reporting. In 2004, she returned to the U.S. and worked as a national reporter at the *St. Petersburg Times* in Florida, traveling the Gulf Coast to document the aftermath of Hurricane Katrina and reporting on disaster, terrorism, and human resilience from Sri Lanka, Indonesia, Russia and the U.K. In 2007, she traveled to Liberia on an International Reporting Project fellowship at the Johns Hopkins University School of Advanced International Studies. Her work has appeared in the *Los Angeles Times*, *The Baltimore Sun*, *The Washington Post Magazine*, and *Slate*, among others. She holds a B.A. in English from Yale University.

DR. SEBASTIAN GORKA is a military affairs fellow at the Foundation for Defense of Democracies, and is an internationally-recognized authority on issues of national security, terrorism, and democratization, having worked on these issues in government and the private and NGO sectors in both Europe and the United States. A graduate of the University of London, he was a Kokkalis Fellow at Harvard's John F. Kennedy School of Government, and holds a Ph.D. in political science from Corvinus University in Budapest. In the past, Dr. Gorka has acted as a consultant to the RAND Corporation's Washington office, and was the first director of the Institute for Transitional Democracy and International Security. After September 11, 2001, he spent four years as an adjunct professor for Terrorism and Security Studies at the George C. Marshall Center in Germany. He has published more than 130 monographs, book chapters, and articles, and is a regular participant in the Department of Defense's Pakistan-Afghanistan Federation Forum and a member of the Strategic Advisers' Group of the Atlantic Council of the United States. The author's views do not necessarily reflect those of any department of the U.S. government. He can be contacted by e-mail at seb.gorka@gmail.com.

SHUJA NAWAZ is the Director of the South Asia Center at the Atlantic Council of the United States in Washington, D.C. He is the author of *Crossed Swords: Pakistan, Its Army, and the Wars Within* (Oxford University Press 2008) and *FATA: A Most Dangerous Place* (CSIS 2009).

JOSHUA T. WHITE is a Research Fellow at the Institute for Global Engagement's Center on Faith & International Affairs, and a Ph.D. candidate at The Johns Hopkins University School of Advanced International Studies (SAIS) in Washington, D.C. His research focuses on Islamic politics, governance, and political stability in South Asia. He spent nearly a year living in Peshawar, Pakistan in 2005-06, and returned to Pakistan in the summers of 2007 and 2008 as a Visiting Research Associate at the Lahore University of Management Sciences. He has presented his findings in numerous academic and policy fora; has testified before the U.S. Congress; has participated in several high-level U.S.-Pakistan Track II strategic dialogues; and has served on U.S.-sponsored election observer delegations to both Pakistan and Bangladesh. He received his M.A. in International Relations from SAIS, and upon graduating received the 2008 Christian A. Herter Award, the school's highest academic honor.

INDEX

FOUNDATION FOR DEFENSE OF DEMOCRACIES

A NONPARTISAN POLICY INSTITUTE DEDICATED EXCLUSIVELY TO PROMOTING PLURALISM, DEFENDING DEMOCRATIC VALUES, AND FIGHTING THE IDEOLOGIES THAT THREATEN DEMOCRACY.

LEADERSHIP COUNCIL

Dr. Paula J. Dobriansky
Fmr. Under Secretary of State for Democracy
and Global Affairs

Steve Forbes
CEO, *Forbes Magazine*

Judge Louis J. Freeh
Fmr. FBI Director

Newt Gingrich
Fmr. Speaker, U.S. House of Representatives

Max M. Kampelman
Fmr. Ambassador

Bill Kristol
Editor, *Weekly Standard*

Senator Joseph Lieberman
(DI-CT) U.S. Senate

Robert C. McFarlane
Fmr. National Security Advisor

R. James Woolsey
Fmr. CIA Director

BOARD OF ADVISORS

Gary Bauer
Representative Eric Cantor
Gene Gately
General P.X. Kelley
Charles Krauthammer
Kathleen Troia "KT" McFarland

Richard Perle
Steven Pomerantz
Oliver "Buck"Revell
Bret Stephens
Hon. Francis J. "Bing" West
Hon. Charles E. Allen

IN MEMORIAM

Jack Kemp
Fmr. Secretary of Housing and Urban
Development

Dr. Jeane J. Kirkpatrick
Fmr. Ambassador to the UN

Clifford D. May
President

Mark Dubowitz
Executive Director

Ambassador Richard W. Carlson
Vice-Chairman

Made in the USA
San Bernardino, CA
24 October 2014